STAND STILL

Stand Still

Finding Balance When the World Turns Upside Down

Terry Hershey

franciscan media®
Cincinnati, Ohio

Unless otherwise indicated, Scripture citations are taken from the *New Revised Standard Version Bible*, copyright ©1989 by the Division of Christian Education of the National Council of Churches of Christ in the U.S.A. and used by permission.

Cover and book design by Mark Sullivan.

Cataloguing in Publication data on file at the Library of Congress

ISBN 978-1-63253-400-2

Published by Franciscan Media
28 W. Liberty St.
Cincinnati, OH 45202
www.FranciscanMedia.org

Printed in the United States of America.
Printed on acid-free paper.
22 23 24 25 26 5 4 3 2 1

Contents

Introduction

What do you do when the/your world feels/turns upside down?

When your world feels unrecognizable and unsettled? When you feel overwhelmed and alone?

It is no surprise that we want answers or solutions. Or, at the very least, some explanations. But wouldn't you know it, none of the answers seem easy or what we had in mind.

In an email late in 2020, someone asked, "What have you been learning during this past year?" And I responded, "More than ever, the invitation to wonder and to savor life in the moment. To be here now." Even when now is challenging, even when now is difficult, even when now is completely upside down.

I write my daily blog, *Sabbath Moment*, because I want to live with a soft heart, to create a place for sanctuary, empathy, inclusion, compassion, and kindness—a space where we are refueled to make a difference. And when life feels upside down, it's not that easy to do. So 2020 was a reset button time for me; I had to find ways to stay spiritually hydrated without my usual activities and speaking engagements. The insights you'll find in this book emerged in that time of global pandemic and lockdown during the COVID-19 crisis. Each chapter begins with a memory flash from that experience. But the insights hold for any time your world, my world, our world turns upside down.

I'll say this: My new congregation helped. A flock of sheep on my morning walk patiently listening to my daily homilies and ramblings. When life feels catawampus, we haven't trusted that we are empowered to witness and savor this life. The sheep helped me do just that. And they reminded me of the invitation to embrace the gift of vicarious joy, to be aware of the communal nature of our journey. When we move from my story, his or her story, to our story, our world becomes bigger. Our horizons expand, keeping us from closed minds and hearts, which are the fuel for fear, paranoia, jealousy—and shame.

But it helps if we see our story as a life-giving invitation, and the permission to embrace a paradigm shift. We forget that our well-being is not at the mercy of life's happenings. We get to choose the lens through which we invite life in. Our well-being is grounded in the power of this paradigm shift. And here's the gift: In our shifting, challenging, uncertain world, we are invited to pay attention to ways that our lives can be recalibrated, grounded in values that allow us to find the sacrament of the present moment.

This is not a cerebral endeavor, as in, "I believe in attentiveness and the sacrament of the present." You see, we are wired to want lives that matter. To be connected. To make a difference. And yes, to spill hope. We are wired to savor the sights and sound of the day. So, here's the deal: When we are present—attentive—we remember and embrace what matters.

This is a book about what we value and where we anchor our well-being. It's about where we park our presence, where we say, "I am here. Here I can give, listen, learn, empathize, grow, forgive, welcome, and invite. Here is where I will discover, uncover, notice, unearth, grasp, appreciate, recognize."

Much derails us. Noise, distraction, an inability to say no, an inability to have boundaries for a healthy self. Our internal worrier will continue to pester us: "What's the secret? How do we actually practice it?" But that is the enigma, isn't it? Life turns left and does somersaults when we least expect it. So, we juggle and we multitask. And we want someone to give us the answers. We want someone to balance it all or give us the list.

Living in the present, fully alive and wholehearted, is not a technique. There is no list. And chances are, we pass by life—the exquisite, the messy, the enchanting, the untidy, the inexplicable—on our way to someplace we think we ought to be. When life throws us a curve that makes our present moment loom larger than anything else, we learn to shift our focus.

There is meaning—consequence, value, import—only when what we believe or teach touches this moment. In other words, it's the small (and specific) stuff that really does matter. Belief is all well and good, but there has to be skin on it—something we touch, see, hear, taste, and smell. The ordinary really is the hiding place for the holy.

On Friday nights I enjoy PBS and Judy Woodruff's conversation with political pundits Mark Shields and David Brooks. One week she asked the question, "What has kept you sane during this pandemic?" I don't recall their answers, but here's my answer. "My best days are when I let my soul catch up."

> An American traveler planned a long safari to Africa. He was a compulsive man, loaded down with maps, timetables, and agendas. Local men had been engaged to carry the cumbersome load of supplies, luggage, and "essential stuff."
>
> On the first morning, they all woke very early and traveled very fast and went very far. On the second morning, they all woke very early and traveled very fast and went very far. On the third morning, they all woke very early and traveled very fast and went very far. And the American seemed pleased. On the fourth morning, the hired men refused to move. They simply sat by a tree.
>
> The American became incensed. "This is a waste of valuable time. Can someone tell me what is going on here?"

> The translator answered, "They are waiting for their souls to catch up with their bodies."

What's at stake here with this sacred necessity of stillness is not another "to do" list, but an invitation to savor the pleasure of slowness, moments of stillness, even silence, letting them work their magic. There is a part of us that protests, "This pandemic has given me a heap plenty of stillness. I'm stir crazy." (In a profound way, the pandemic has reminded us that physical dormancy or inactivity doesn't mean our spirit or brain is not in overdrive.) We need to pause in such a way that our souls catch up.

In her book *The Solace of Open Spaces*, Gretel Ehrlich talks about the concept that space can heal. That space—created by silence—represents sanity. Mercy: what a gift! Silence can be a fullness, rather than a void. It can allow the mind to run through its paces without any need for justification. It can let us recover—grab hold of—those parts of ourselves that have been scattered, disparate, throughout the week. To sit still is a spiritual endeavor.

To stand still is to practice Sabbath—meaning literally, to rest. To stop. To savor uncluttered time. To be gentle with yourself. And yes, to waste time with God. The bottom line? I'm no longer chasing what I assume will fill empty spaces in order to make me something I am not. Replenishment begins here: "I am enough."

In our Western mindset, living in the present becomes a staged event—staged to be "spiritual," as if this is something we must orchestrate or arrange. No wonder we sit stewing in the juices of our self-consciousness ("Am I present? What am I doing right or wrong?"), all the while missing the point.

As long as the present moment needs to be staged in order to be enough, we live from scarcity, not sufficiency. We have forgotten the gift of enough. So, it's *sankofa* time. *Sankofa* (in the Akan Twi language of Ghana) is associated with the proverb, "*Se wo were fi na wosankofa a yenkyi*," which translates, "It is not wrong to go back for that which you have forgotten." Yes.

More than ever we need sustenance, places of sanity and restoration. When we've been through—or are going through—a time of upheaval, we need *sankofa*: the permission to give ourselves the gift of stillness and sanctuary. To remember the sufficiency that is alive and well inside. Noise (distraction) makes it easy to forget, to see only what we're "missing." But here's the deal: When I see only scarcity, I miss the fact that every single one of us has been gifted with creativity, abundance, heart, love, passion, gentleness, helpfulness, caring, kindness, tenderness, restoration, and a shoulder to lean on (for crying or for dancing, depending on the mood at the time). Stillness and sanctuary: This is the paradigm of sufficiency.

I'm glad you've joined me on this journey, just "walking one another home," as spiritual teacher Ram Dass would say.

It is in our DNA to be replenished. Refueled. Renewed. It is in our DNA to be emotionally and spiritually hydrated. Which is why the times when our emotional and spiritual tanks feel dry or empty, we're eager to make things right again. Hoping we can find some kind of normal.

I confess that I'm not a competent list maker. As a "P" on the Myers-Briggs test, I think "deadline" means "time to get started." I might have a list, but I've probably misplaced it. Even so, looking back over what I wrote and thought during our upheaval year, I realized that I did, in fact, practice a list.

- The power of pause; the ability to stand still.
- The gift of self-care; be gentle with yourself.
- The gift of enough; live each day from gratitude.

- The permission to pay attention; the gift of curiosity, wonder, and awe.
- The sacrament of the present moment.
- The gift of "we"; no one is on this journey alone.

When someone asks me why I write, I say it's to practice and internalize this list. Our list is not an assignment or test to pass. This isn't a contest or a beauty pageant. This is an invitation to embrace and to use what is already alive and well inside of each and every one of us. And yes, when we're undone, uncertain, and dehydrated, it is easy to forget or find ourselves derailed.

What do you do when the world turns upside down? You hit the pause button. And you remember that none of us is on this journey alone. Join me as we walk, talk, learn, and grow. Join me as we remember that which we've forgotten in our hurry and fear. Join me as we refuel and heal.

Chapter One

Preaching to the Sheep

You'll permit me to smile at a wonderful irony. This email from a reader in 2019: "I'd love a day with no obligations, to sit and read and ponder and wander and peruse and just be." (Be careful what you wish for.)

I walk every morning. A few miles around Fisher Pond here on Vashon Island. Not far from my house, I pass a neighbor's field, home to a flock of sheep. Today, I stopped and talked with them. Two of the mamas have new twins. Yes, they are adorable. This morning, it felt like church, so I gave them a little homily. Not too long. Seven minutes or so.

I tell them that some days I don't want to read the news. At least not until after lunch. I tell them our world convulses with uncertainty and anxiety. I tell them that people are on the edge (money, jobs, bills, family members sick or dying), and you may never know the whole story. I tell them I don't know what to write for *Sabbath Moment*; I have trouble finding the words. They stare, seeming to listen to me, but with a passive gaze.

Here's what I do know: They did my heart good. I watched the little ones cuddling and nestling and sheltering up to their mamas, so very glad to be alive. I go on with my walk carrying these gifts from my morning congregation, living vicariously and wholeheartedly through their joy, and very glad to be alive.

I'm back on my porch with coffee. I'm glad you're here. Pull up a chair. I am aware that some of my anxiety is from the temptation that, in order to inspire and encourage, one must find remedies tidily packaged in mental pictures. It's just that life doesn't work that way. In the midst of competing anxieties, I want to fully embrace the gift of the sacrament of the present moment.

After time with my "congregation," I walk my garden. Lilacs are budded. The shrubs lean (or bow in reverence?) from the weight of last night's heavy rain. Here's my prayer: I want to be awake, in this life, in this moment, the very one I am living today. Precarious? Indeed. Which is why this life is so much more precious.

There is power in words. We used to talk about the need to free up time. Now, there's a paradigm shift; we can embrace time as a sacred gift. I'll tell you what replenished me today.

The sheep didn't ask about my bank account or bills not getting paid, or when and if I would work (travel) again. Or, about when life would go back to normal. Of course, I don't know when that will be. While I'm waiting for "normal," the sacred is still alive and well. And the ordinary is the hiding place of the holy.

- Human connection is alive and well.
- Empathy and compassion are alive and well.
- Beauty and gladness are alive and well.
- Sanctuary is alive and well.
- Ministry is alive and well.
- Spontaneous gestures of kindness are alive and well.
- Music from the heart is alive and well.

Transformation (conversion) brings with it an extraordinary gift. I was raised in a religious tradition that mandated conversion, which punched my ticket for the afterlife. I was frequently asked what I would do if I died today. I was never once asked what I would do if I lived.

But what if conversion is about living this life, today, with my whole heart?

"We are healed of a suffering only by experiencing it to the full," Marcel Proust wrote. So we wake up to this fragile and exquisitely beautiful life and embrace the sacred present. When I'm not preoccupied (held captive by angst), I notice, I pay attention, I see. And in taking ownership of my life—this life—I am available. Not frightened by scarcity, I'm not enticed to ask, "What do I need today?" Rather, I can ask, "What do others need today?" You see, I have both resources and assets to give: a listening ear, empathy, a calm demeanor, a shout-out to a friend, words of consolation.

Chapter Two

Our Strength Is Grounded in Humility

New Year resolutions. I could tell you that I'm going to aim high: Eliminate worry. Or I could aim low: promise to cut down my emoji use. But my gut tells me that the truth fits this one: I will read the manual about inner peace... just as soon as I can find it. If I'm honest, I can tell you I drag my heels, as (to my detriment) head-in-the-sand has served me well. But I do know this: In 2020, I will keep telling stories. Because stories keep us sane. And I will speak honestly, from my heart. A disconcerting commitment in a world where we're not sure where truth parks itself, and perception too often wins.

—January 1, 2020

Truth, for me, must begin with my own pessimism and sadness, knowing that when I let go of the manic tug of urgency, I'll be face-to-face with the demons I've kept at bay. I'm still afraid to be grateful for such a gift—this sacred and messy self. So I give myself grief, as if my value is predicated on keeping score, my mental calculator at the ready.

"So, you're sixty-five?" the young man asks, incredulous.

"I am indeed," I tell him. He scrutinizes me.

"Wow. What are you going to do with your life now?"

It never hurts to begin your New Year with a come-to-Jesus moment. Certain questions give us a run for our money. And we take a moment to breathe. I take the high road and tell him I'll tidy up, going through piles of stuff that have been assembling over the years. Only some of it is actual, physical stuff.

His look tells me all I need to know, "So that's what old people have to look forward to?"

I call my friend Ed for help. "I don't know what to say," he tells me. "But telling the truth is a good place to begin. We live in a world that needs honesty without pat answers."

So, I spend the week juggling the young man's question in my mind. And here's my answer: I choose to live fully awake and unafraid, knowing that strength is grounded in humility.

Standing in line at our local bank, a friend asks, "Do you have any new books or CDs available?"

A teller overhears and says, "You sell CDs? I didn't know you sang."

"I don't," I tell her. "It frightens young children."

"Then what's on your CDs?" she asks.

"They are talks," I say. "Workshops."

"What kind of material?"

"Motivational," I answer.

"Oh," she sounds surprised. "You never look motivated to me."

Maybe I come across better on audio. Who knew? I leave the bank laughing, and humbled in that good sort of way, wondering about what I need to alter for an appropriate demeanor. Or whether I wear my discontent and disquiet a little too conspicuously. Have I resorted to a sort of numbness?

Besides, what do motivated (invested, involved, difference-making) people look like? It's a real question. In one episode of *On Being*, Krista Tippett takes a listener's question, "How can we be present to what's happening in the world without giving in to despair and hopelessness?"

How can I be present (or motivated)? What does it mean to be at home in my own skin? Sadly, we find plenty of ways to reinforce the restrictive narrative that we are not enough. So let's begin here. It's not advice (or resolutions) we need, but permission. Permission to honor our real self. The gift of this self (this beautiful and broken self) is sufficient. And the gift of being real spills to those around us.

Consider another story from *On Being*, in which singer-songwriter Joe Henry says that as he's grown older, he's gained the ability to see himself as complete.

> I think when you're young, you're inclined to believe—invited to believe that yet you couldn't have done anything significant enough to own an identity, a point of view. And then you get to a point when you're just like, "Well, I think I'm basically who I am now.... And there's a liberation that comes with getting to a point where you think, I'm not waiting for that next great shoe to drop." Both the shoes may be laying here.

I love the metaphor. This life we are waiting for? It is already here. We start with this self (not our resolution or aspiration self) to give, care, try, love, hope, endeavor, fall down and get up again. To show up every day. Accepting and owning the worth and value of this self is no longer about stereotypes, or the need to fit in, or shame about regret. There is relief and freedom knowing that the music matches the words.

The irony is this: Freedom to change and learn and stretch grows in the soil of that affirmation. Why is this so easy to forget? When I start with the narrative that this Terry is not enough (not motivated or striving), it's no surprise that I worry about appearance or image. Or play the victim. If we feel that we are not enough, we run from those places that are uncomfortable or awkward (scolding ourselves for what we "should" be). We run from times of unraveling, or those times when we are clearly not "motivated."

Feeling that we're not enough, we live in a perpetual state of tinkering (stuck in the world of "someday and if-only"), never at home in our own skin. So despair may not be far away.

One friend told me this week, "Where I am right now in my life is not fun. I think I could just die, and it would be OK." I understand and I know those thoughts, when I believe I have no options, or am too tired to figure it out, or the weight of life seems too heavy. We may see it coming (this weight), or it may take us by surprise (kind of a tsunami).

But whether the knife falls on the melon, or the melon falls on the knife, it's still the melon that suffers. Not unlike our heart.

The insidious reminder that we are not enough has always been an opportunity to hammer guilt. As in, why haven't I done enough? What's the best I can accomplish and be productive? Lord knows, it is essential to have something to show for my day. (I'm as tempted as the next guy by the a sense of well-being that comes from having a clean desk.)

Some people take exception to my talk about the power of pause, living in the present moment, and the art of doing nothing. They don't like the idea of "wasting time." But there's a difference between wasting time and just being bored: Wasting time really is intentional. You are, literally, spending time. On clouds, or lilies, or naps, or silence, or prayer, or providing a generous spirit, or coffee with friends (even if on Zoom), or listening to someone's story, or caring for a flock of birds, or watching your cats fight it out for the best spot on the couch. Which means that you are not mortgaging your time or your life on any old distraction merely out of boredom.

When you do pause and pay attention, there is an internal recalibration. While nothing is "added" to your life, there is a new awareness of the light that is within. Let's call it our new internal wealth account.

As long as success is measured by keeping score, we lose track of most everything that makes us human and, therefore, glad to be alive.

- Small gestures of kindness.
- Acts of inclusion or community to someone left out, or someone on the fringes.
- Extending a hand of healing or acceptance to someone who hurts.
- Reveling in the gifts of the senses and being present.
- Resting in a moment of gratitude (say, an English rose bloom that makes you weak in the knees).
- Sharing laughter, a smile, camaraderie, dancing, or joy (or all of the above).

In an episode of *The West Wing*, C.J. Cregg (the new White House chief of staff) is wired, tense, and distracted. Danny (her love interest) shows up, in the middle of the workday, at her White House office, "to take her for a walk." She consents (but not without a fight, you know, "so much to do"). On the walk, she fidgets and asks, "So, what was so important?"

Danny: "What?"
C.J.: "You said it was important."
Danny: "It's this, the walk, the day."
C.J.: "That's it?"
Danny: "Yeah, you're locked up in that building all day long, it's gorgeous out here, I thought you should see it."
C.J.: "...I have a packed day. This is really sweet, but today is not the time for it."

It made me laugh out loud. Sure, I want to live this moment, to be mindful of the sacred, to savor and take delight—but this is not the day for it. As if there is a special day for it? For all I've written about the sacrament of the present moment, one of my choice mutterings is, "I'm in favor of living in the present, just not this one."

Remember when Jesus said, "The kingdom of God is among you" (Luke 17:21)? Meaning "it's right now, in the midst of you, right here." Meaning, this ordinary moment (whether tranquil or untidy or befuddling or exasperating) can be a container of grace, the sacrament of the blessed present. Meaning, the visible and the invisible are one. The Celts spoke about such experiences as "thin places," times and places when and where the sacred is almost palpable.

Yes, I get it. I *teach* it. And yet my mind easily convinces me of the opposite. I can miss what is right in front of me. When our minds tell us that the kingdom is still yet to be, somewhere in the future, we give up who we are today for who we think we should be. I understand that distraction and exhaustion may be our new normal. However, if I live each day from that paradigm, I'm unable to give, care, listen, reconcile, mend from my whole heart. Because when I'm away from the present, I'm not at peace.

In this culture where economic value bests intrinsic value, we are owned by narratives that diminish us. We have forgotten our DNA.

"What has been lost is the true beholding of the light from the inner eyes," wrote John Scotus Eriugena, a ninth-century Irish philosopher. Grace is given to heal that inner sight, to open our eyes again to the goodness that is deep within us, for God is within us. The grace of Christ restores us to our original simplicity.

William Sloane Coffin elaborates, "Of God's love we can say two things: it is poured out universally for everyone from the Pope to the loneliest wino on the planet and secondly, God's love doesn't seek value, it creates value. It is not because we have value that we are loved, but because we are loved that we have value. Our value is a gift, not an achievement."

Love (value or meaning) is not something you produce or achieve or acquire. It is not something that you even have. Love is something that has you. So we surrender. Now, grounded in humility (with no appetite to be somebody we are not), love will soften our hearts, shrinking rage and saying no to contempt. "When we are in touch with our blessedness," Henri Nouwen reminds us, "we can then bless other people." And in that blessing, "we...awaken from the illusion of our separateness" (Thich Nhat Hanh).

We are not on this journey alone.

In the story of Theseus and the Minotaur (a tale from ancient Greece), after Theseus has slain the beast in the center of the underground labyrinth, he guides himself back to the surface by a length of thread given him by Ariadne, the king's daughter, retracing his steps through the dark maze of tunnels. So what is that thread for you? Where are those sanctuaries (people or places) that help you remember who you are (that you are enough) and those parts of you that have not yet gone to sleep? Where (and how) do you give yourself the permission to hang onto that thread and embrace the present?

Chapter Three

Life Turned Upside Down

This week, our local news was very painful. The first coronavirus death in the U.S. happened here in the Seattle area. Yes, it is real. I loved the responses from our local officials: calm. And the best line of defense is to pay attention to our immune system. It reminds me that in a real way, being present is an immunity against exasperation, exhaustion, and detachment.

—March 2, 2020

Remember that even when life turns upside down, we all have the capacity to care. Let us raise a glass and tell stories in grateful awe for ordinary people who in ordinary ways make our world kinder, more caring, and more compassionate, one heart and one life at a time.

A mother begins her weekend breakfast routine, pulling ingredients from the refrigerator. Omelets are on the family menu this morning. Before she knows it, her two-year-old daughter has climbed a chair and is now sitting on the kitchen counter.

"Mama, can I help?"

"Of course, honey."

The little girl removes an egg from the carton, and does her best imitation of momma, cracking eggs into the bowl. The first egg breaks on the rim, half staying in the bowl; the other half of the egg plops onto the counter and is now sliding down the front of the cupboards.

Undeterred, and delighted to be cooking breakfast with her mother—"Look Mama, I'm cooking," she squeals—she smashes another egg against the bowl's rim, and then another.

After the fourth egg, her mother barks in exasperation, "Noooo, honey, this is not a good idea. Not right now!"

I'm smiling, in part because I can feel the mother's exasperation, and more so because I'm not the one in the kitchen. (There are moments in parenting when, regardless of the experts, there are, quite literally, no words.)

Chances are good that any helpful two-year-old will break some eggs. At some juncture in my life, I will need to choose. Do I want a tidy kitchen or a life-giving relationship with people significant in my life (even the ones that include or even create the mess)? Chances are good that the script I had in mind will be mercifully and humanely altered. But it's not just a kitchen, is it? Or parenting skills. It's about owning up to the script I carry, expectations or assumptions about what makes life real. Somehow, we've swallowed the notion that real life happens after there is tidiness, or after the cleanup, or after the enlightenment, or after the script is edited. And when I live by that script, it chips away at my reserve of hope.

Here's the question: What do we do with life's script edits (whether personal or national)?

It is true (and not surprising) that chaos (messes, disarray) unnerves some people more than others. (My OCD kicks in. Some of you can relate, those like me who are just plain wonderfully wired funny.)

Our need for tidiness as a condition of well-being comes in many forms:

- If there are questions, we want answers.
- If there are struggles, we make resolutions.
- If we experience unsightly emotions, we apologize ("I'm sorry," we will tell others, wiping away the tears).

- If there are impediments, we want no loose ends.
- If there is a blunder or muddle, we are given to a compulsion to explain. Or blame. Sometimes even in a ballistic way.

This is important: Crises can undo us, that is true, but if we attach a crisis to something we can attack ("the little girl broke the eggs on purpose"), we live defensively and reactively. But what if life is bigger than avoiding broken eggs? Or even tidying up? What if caring and kindness draw from a different reservoir?

Remember *sankofa* ("It is not wrong to go back for that which you have forgotten"). Before advice or "should," *sankofa* is an intentional pause to renew ourselves to the values we cherish. To reclaim our voice.

Think of this: Broken eggs can be an invitation to honor the truth that, as Helen Keller said, "Alone we can do so little; together we can do so much." And here's the good news: The values we cherish are not arbitrary. They are reciprocal. In other words, when we honor them, they, in turn, fuel us.

"The more alert we become to the blessing that flows into us through everything we touch, the more our own touch will bring blessing," Br. David Steindl-Rast reminds us. A gift: When we see broken eggs, we can say, "It's time for a blessing." So let's start with what we know: Life is about presence (even with broken eggs).

We have become skilled at (and consumed by) emotional multitasking. It's not just the tidy part that motivates us. We want the assurance that it brings. You know: Now that things are in order, I can enjoy life more. While we are focusing our energy on the perfect picture (or omelet or relationship or child or church or faith or life script), our minds are already into the future, and because of that, we cannot be Here. Now. Present. This sacred moment. Yes, sacred even in the uncertainty and the pain. And when we can see the gift of the child beyond the mess, we will respond from a place of generosity and hopefulness.

Chapter Four

Rearranging Our Priorities

This week, my mind raced. Unsettled. And I know I am not alone. You know the world has tilted slightly when Costco is out of toilet paper.

—March 9, 2020

"What do you do to stay sane?" a reader asked me. "I'm unnerved. There's too much on my plate. And my bandwidth can't handle it." And I knew she was talking about more than just the coronavirus. Whenever I get a question, I confess that my temptation is to find answers that erase anxiety. Instead, I say, "Let me tell you two stories."

> During the Iraq War, a five-year-old boy watches the news with his father.
>
> The boy keeps asking, "How big is this war? How did it start? What is war? Why are so many families on the TV so sad?"
>
> The father tries to explain why countries go to war, why some people think wars are necessary, and other people believe that wars are wrong. But the boy keeps asking the same questions, night after night.
>
> Finally, the father listens. And hears the real question.
>
> He holds his son tight and says to him, "You don't have to worry. We are safe here. Dad will keep you safe. And our family will

> be safe, and we will do whatever we can to help keep other families safe."
>
> After his dad spoke, the boy became peaceful, because it was the reassurance his heart had been asking for.

So often we're looking not for factual explanations but for a sense that the world is turning and we're safe in the midst of chaos and confusion.

In her book *Writing Down the Bones*, Natalie Goldberg wrote about a three-month visit to Jerusalem and her Israeli landlady, a woman in her fifties. The woman called a repairman to fix her broken TV. It took the repairman four visits to fix the screen.

> "But you knew even before he came the first time what was wrong," Natalie told her. "He could have brought the correct tube and fixed it immediately."
>
> The landlady looked at her in astonishment. "Yes, but then we couldn't have had a relationship, sat and drunk tea and discussed the progress of the repairs." Of course, Goldberg writes, "the goal was not to fix the machine but to have a relationship. To make a connection—to touch, to see, to listen, to discover, to drink from the well of the day's gladness."

Both stories make us want to ask: How, then, do we measure? What is essential? How do we decide (honor) the things that really matter?

I like the idea of rearranging our priorities. Getting our ducks in a row. And it is easy to resonate with the goal part. It provides needed ballast for that fragment of our psyche that requires closure. So, we're all-in. And if it comes with an easy-to-follow checklist, all the better. (Which is all well and good until someone changes the list.)

But what if measuring is not even about the list? Is it possible that we are asking the wrong questions?

The question is almost never the question. And more often than not, fixing the broken TV is not the goal. There are plenty of reasons for uncertainty and the need for both answers and connection or comfort. But I know that when my immune system is compromised, I am susceptible to any number of things that unravel and derail. This isn't because I have failed some test. Or am in some way inadequate. Heavens, no. It's because I'm simply not what Meister Eckhart called my "best and truest" self.

I love this bit of wisdom from another *On Being* episode:

> In many Muslim cultures, when you want to ask them how they're doing, you ask: in Arabic, *Kayf haal-ik?* or, in Persian, *Haal-e shomaa chetoreh?* How is your *haal*? What is this *haal* that you inquire about? It is the transient state of one's heart. In reality, we ask, "How is your heart doing at this very moment, at this breath?" When I ask, "How are you?" that is really what I want to know. I am not asking how many items are on your to-do list, nor asking how many items are in your inbox. I want to know how your heart is doing, at this very moment. Tell me. Tell me your heart is joyous, tell me your heart is aching, tell me your heart is sad, tell me your heart craves a human touch. Examine your own heart, explore your soul, and then tell me something about your heart and your soul.

"Being in touch with the heart tells us the quality of our existence, tells us how we recognize the truth," Russ Hudson writes. "The heart also is the place where we know who we really are."

I love that the father (in the first story) stepped back and asked, "How can I pay attention to the heart?"

Our invitation today? To pause. To make space to be present. To pay attention to our heart. Presence is the medicine. There is power in that medicine, as we live honestly with our fears and questions and spill care, kindness, and hope. People have told me that pain will be my teacher. They just didn't tell me what I would learn. I can tell you this: With pain (or uncertainty or waylaid plans or fractures of the heart or broken TV sets), it is too easy to focus only on the fixing. Or the correct path. And in my urgency for resolve, I can miss the spirit of life. Today, Natalie's landlady gives my heart a jolt.

Chapter Five

We're Not on This Journey Alone

The world has shifted. And the pain and sacrifice are real. But here's what I know: Life didn't stop. And the earth still turns. As I write these words, the moon, waning gibbous, smiles brightly through the fir branches on the two-hundred-foot, one-hundred-year-old trees near my house.

—March 15, 2020

I won't pretend. Sometimes I just want to close my eyes. But fear doesn't help any one of us.

So pull up a chair, my friend. It is porch chat time. I have plenty of chairs, even if only virtual. I'll pour you a coffee. I made plenty. It's the good stuff, no church-hour coffee here. It's early, but I have wine if you prefer. And let's talk, shall we?

Fear is not easy to avoid with the tsunami of data. And cognitive dissonance is alarming. In our circle, there is no room for fear or alarm or panic. And for anyone who trucks in falsehoods, please stop it. Let us remember: None of us is on this journey alone.

Many of us have been mentally ticking off moments in our lifetime when our world changed. Personal, mostly: births, weddings, deaths. And times when our world tilted: President Kennedy's assassination, 9/11, Hurricane Katrina.

The power here is that this time of pandemic is truly collective. We are, literally, in the same boat. We pay a price if we don't have these sit-downs, even if they're virtual. It's essential to do our part to slow fear and mute voices of alarm and panic.

When life is upside down, we easily forget the fundamental truth that we live from sufficiency, not scarcity. Even in times of distress. At the beginning of the lockdown in 2020, church was canceled, March Madness was canceled, public gatherings were canceled. Author Jamie Tworkowski posted this on Twitter:

> Conversations will not be cancelled.
> Relationships will not be cancelled.
> Love will not be cancelled.
> Songs will not be cancelled.
> Reading will not be cancelled.
> Self-care will not be cancelled.
> Hope will not be cancelled.

And I would add,

Gardening will not be cancelled.

Watching the moonlight filter through the trees will not be cancelled.

And lifting one another's spirits will not be cancelled.

May we lean into the good stuff that remains.

The sacrament of the present moment will still anchor us, center us, calm us. No matter what else is going on around us, it invites us to pay attention to the things that really matter.

Here's a list:

- Pause. Stand still. Breathe.
- Reach out to loved ones, friends, acquaintances, strangers: A word of understanding, encouragement, even just a smile.
- Savor beauty wherever you notice it.
- Practice gratitude. For everything. The good, the bad, the difficult, the joyous, the challenging, the reassuring.

- Care for those who are vulnerable. And let others care for you.

This is not a time to castigate. This is not a time to eschew responsibility. In fact, I do take responsibility to make choices that will fuel hope, consolation, calm, and tranquility.

Transformative events will be hard. So, whatever love is in your heart, nurture it, develop it, grow it, spread it. Spread it to your family, but don't stop there. Spread it beyond. It is the only force that can heal our broken world. And don't let your heart be infected with selfishness.

Chapter Six

We Were Made for This

Yes there is fear.
Yes there is isolation.
Yes there is panic buying.
Yes there is sickness.
Yes there is even death.
But,
They say that in Wuhan after so many years of noise
You can hear the birds again. (Br. Richard Hendrick)

—March 23, 2020

Change messes with us. I wish it weren't so. Change messes with the tidy (manageable and predictable) script we tote for mental security. About the way life should be.

"Now, we need to think outside the box," someone posted online.

"What box?" another wondered.

Yes, indeed. It wouldn't hurt to know where to begin.

I'm glad you're back on the patio with me. Pull up a chair. Let me pour you a coffee. Let's talk. Here's what I know: When life is only about what we possess, or what we have lost, we miss seeing and hearing the truth about who we are at our core. We've lost the empowerment that comes from knowing that what is at our core (compassion, generosity, kind-heartedness, our capacity for connection) is greater than whatever change confronts or challenges us.

In other words, we have forgotten our best selves. We have forgotten that we were made for this, one soul helping another.

"What will life be when this is past us, back to normal?" someone posted.

Ahhh, it's normal we're looking for, is it? (No wonder we're prone to panic, and seem to double down with fear. And from my experience, that's never fun.)

With my life on hold, I miss the invitation and the gift of life. Today. True, in the life I have now, there are many things I cannot do. However, in the life I have now, I can look for daily miracles.

- I can savor gifts of gladness and grace abounding.
- I can find beauty and pass these gifts on.
- In the life I have now, I can see the sacred present as the hiding place for the holy.
- I can do whatever possible to remember that we are on this journey together.
- I can give to those where pain and fear hit hardest.
- I can trust the healing power of empathy.
- I can send virtual hugs.
- I can listen, and invite music and heartfelt passion.
- And I will not allow inconvenience to be my measuring stick for daily choices.

"I wish it need not have happened in my time," said Frodo.

"So do I," said Gandalf, "and so do all who live to see such times. But that is not for them to decide. All we have to decide is what to do with the time that is given us." (J.R.R. Tolkien, *The Fellowship of the Ring*)

Yes. We were made for this, one soul helping another. Here's what I'm learning: Some gifts don't show up when life seems easier. When the noise is louder and the lights are brighter, it's easy to miss the gifts. When that happens, we live reactively (demeaning, blaming, in denial), which helps no one.

"We're going to be changed," someone else posted online.

I hope so. What a marvelous gift. As humans, we have the capacity to change and adapt. (Why do we seem surprised that disasters evoke, invite, and awaken the extraordinary power of kindness?)

Let me refill your coffee cup. And let's talk about ways we can honor both our emotional and physical immune system and those who are vulnerable around us.

Pause. Literally. Make space for self-care. To reflect. To let your soul catch up.

Count me in. There are many things I can let go of: my need to be impervious, and my preoccupation with any compulsion to be in control. Vulnerable? Yes. Scared? A little. Still with the capacity to spill light, calm, consolation, and hope? Absolutely.

We are connected. Every single one of us.

"Whatever affects one directly, affects all indirectly. I can never be what I ought to be until you are what you ought to be. This is the interrelated structure of reality," Martin Luther King Jr. reminds us.

I'm reading a great book, *Eating the Sun: Small Musings on a Vast Universe* by Ella Frances Sanders, and loved this:

> Trees are also seemingly able to distinguish their own roots from those of other species, and even those of their relatives. They share food and help to nourish their competitors when they are sick or struggling (in winter an aspen will likely not do as well as a conifer, so the conifer lends a hand), and all this apparently for no other reason than that living becomes much easier when you're helping others, rather than simply ensuring your own survival.

Yes. We were made for this, one soul helping another. So, where do we begin? Know that life is precious. Savor your day. Let a sense of wonder find you. It can happen in many forms. Linger. Drink in. Savor. And share.

Chapter Seven

The Gentle Hands of Grace

On my walk this morning, I talk with my new congregation, the sheep. "It's Palm Sunday," I tell them. "You know, Holy Week." But they give me the look reminding me that for them, every week is a Holy Week, so my enthusiasm doesn't register. Unsure of their faith, I tell them that Passover begins at sundown on Wednesday. And then I remember the part about the lamb in the Passover story and decide to stick with Holy Week.

—*April 5, 2020*

I explain to the sheep that Holy Week is a big deal, our "so this is what it's all about" week. We wait all year for this week. And this year, I tell them, it reminds us of our yearning for normal. (Thinking, as I say the words, "but there's nothing normal about this year. And this definitely wasn't the 'box' we ordered.")

My favorite story, *The Road to Emmaus*, happens at the end of Holy Week, and is about coming face-to-face with a reality we didn't order, and yet, being transformed forever.

"When we are willing to be transformed, we stop wasting time theorizing, projecting, denying, or avoiding our own ego resistance," Richard Rohr writes. In other words, we let go of those boxes of "certainty" that are meant to protect us.

I like the way my good friend Ed Kilbourne tells the story. Ed always tells this story guitar in hand. And since I can't sing, or play guitar, I tell it my way, sitting on the patio with a glass of wine in hand.

One day Jesus was walking along the shoulder of a highway with his thumb out—hitchhiking. And it wasn't because of a lack of transportation. I think Jesus may have been up to something.

A couple in a pickup truck pulled over and offered him a ride. He climbed in. Since they didn't know him, they went right back to the conversation they were having before they stopped. This gave Jesus his chance. To pay attention, to listen in. And they were talking about it. About what had happened in the city they had just left. A local hero, a man who had been welcomed to town with all kinds of excitement, a big parade even, just days earlier, had been killed. Executed. He was caught in some kind of political religious crossfire. This hero was dead. And these two travelers were sad and confused.

I can just imagine those two now, talking away, Jesus leaning against the passenger window looking out at the countryside, trying not to smile, as he listened in. Because they were talking about him. To my way of thinking, Jesus just plain blew his chance at the biggest "ta-da" in history. As they rode along in the pickup, the couple were talking about him. They thought he was dead. They'd lost all hope. But Jesus didn't let on. No "ta-da". They didn't recognize him. Figure that one out.

I think it's important. He did give them clues as they rode along, but he didn't tell them. He let them go on with their questions and their grief. It wasn't until later—in fact, it wasn't until that night at supper—while they were waiting for the waitress to get back with their orders that Jesus reached into the little basket in the middle of the table.

It wasn't until he took a package of crackers and tore it open. It wasn't until he took bread and broke it, and handed them each a piece, that they looked at him and said, "Oh, my God!"'And he was. All along. It was him all along.

And, you know, it's been that way ever since. No "ta-da." No "Supergod." No magical mystical Being that suddenly appears on the scene to divert the course of history and make every ending a happy one. No hands to stop the bullets, no one with superpowers to defeat disease and death. No X-ray vision to see through ignorance or despair.

We make our way down the road, thinking we're alone. But then, time after time, it has happened. It will happen again. The Moment. The coming of the Light, the dawn.

And just as it was that night long ago sitting around that table at the end of the road, there is a clear awareness, a history-changing revelation. A revelation that changes your history. The eyes of your eyes open. And you recognize him. You know. Yes. And a voice comes from somewhere in you, "Oh, my God." And as he was that night with those two, he is still and always, in this and every moment, God. With us.

The holy is not confined or restricted to what we call "normal."

- My eyes are open to the sacrament of the present moment, knowing that the ordinary is the hiding place for the holy.
- My eyes are open to the sacred; in compassionate gestures and hospitality and small heroes and big virtual hugs.
- My eyes are open to the deep river running in each of us.
- My eyes are open to hope found in clarity with no need for arrogance, cruelty, fighting, or paranoia.
- My eyes are open to the invitation to give up the control that I clutched.

I can freely admit that the boxes we put life in (our expectations and our ways to manage) are inadequate.

So, I tell the sheep that having your world shaken isn't a bad thing. Scary, yes. But transformation is closer than we know.

Spirituality is not about a lottery ticket to the next life, but a front-row-center ticket to this one. "Take care of the now for the sake of tomorrow," advises Pope Francis. How do we do that? Our values, those at our core (gentleness, humility, charity, interior simplicity) tether us.

Count me in. I want to take care of now, reinforcing, nourishing, and replenishing that core.

So, join me on the patio. The coffee is on.

"Interruptions" can indeed bring pain, irritation, discomfort. Some of it imagined (toilet paper). Some of it very real (no job, lost loved ones, health care gone, health care workers strained, "attending" a funeral on Zoom). None of that can be diminished. Even so, our invitation doesn't change. In Joseph Campbell's words: "We must be willing to let go of the life we've planned, so as to have the life that is waiting for us."

To be replenished is to be reminded of what is true, of the values that tether us. This is not just someone saying, "You'll be OK." To be replenished is to know, at our core, that we are home and we are safe.

Now we have something to draw on. Which means we have something to give. This sanctuary is not just for solace, but also indispensable as a deterrent. In other words, we build immunity: to not be as easily susceptible to fear, or at the mercy of every threat. We can do this because there are two gentle hands of grace that hold us, no matter what. Let us honor that capacity (inner core), fueled by sufficiency and not scarcity.

We need to honor our capacity for mindfulness. To embrace now and the sacrament of the present moment.

There is a scene in the movie *The Shawshank Redemption* when Andy locks himself in the warden's office, puts a record on the turntable, and sets the prison intercom microphone near the speaker. The music pervades and suffuses the entire prison. Red, the narrator, says:

> I have no idea to this day what those two Italian ladies were singing about. Truth is, I don't want to know. Some things are best left unsaid. I'd like to think they were singing about something so beautiful it can't be expressed in words and makes your heart ache because of it. I tell you, those voices soared higher and farther than anybody in a gray place dares to dream. It was like some beautiful bird flapped into our drab little cage and made those walls dissolve away, and for the briefest of moments, every last man in Shawshank felt free.

Let us take care of the now. "Don't miss the opportunities you have to sit down, without having to worry or think about doing anything. Lay down your burdens, your worries, and your projects. Just sit and feel that you are alive. Sit with your son, your daughter, your partner, your friend. That's enough to be happy," says Thich Nhat Hanh.

We need to honor our capacity for humility. "All the truly transformed people I have ever met are characterized by what I would call radical humility," Richard Rohr writes. "They are deeply convinced that they are drawing from another source; they are simply an instrument. Their genius is not their own; it is borrowed. They end up doing generative and expansive things precisely because they do not take first or final responsibility for their gift; they don't worry too much about their failures, nor do they need to promote themselves. Their life is not their own, yet at some level they know that it has been given to them as a sacred trust."

This has been a good time for pondering. Which works out, as pondering is a life-giving avocation of mine. I remember different times in my life when I was on the road to accomplishment or success, which meant becoming "somebody." There have been so many races that consumed me: to be ahead (which always meant busy), to find perfection, to be in control, be liked or to be loved, to collect trinkets that provoked envy. These were races (ways to see life) that did not nourish or honor the values at my core. And did not trust the gentle hands of grace.

There was, however, a side effect: I became cynical, played the victim, nursed regret, and felt undone by comparison. Now, as I "recollect myself" and take care of now, keep putting oil in the lamp, and rest in the gentle hands of grace, I can say, "Thank you, but I don't need that race anymore."

Chapter Eight

An Invitation to Make Space

On my walk this morning, I ask my congregation, the sheep, "Any advice on what to say to people with anxiety during a pandemic?"

"What do you say during 'normal' times?" their look asked.

"Let's sit a spell on the porch and listen to the birds, maybe wander the garden and smell the flowers, and savor the day," I tell them.

"So, why would you change that?" They chew and stare at me. And a light bulb turns on. The relief we are seeking is connected to an internal switch, not an external one.

—April 27, 2020

Just for the record, "normal" has never been on my list of goals, let alone an aspiration. Although, looking back, it would be easy to guess otherwise. I contorted myself to look the part. After all, what would other people think? Honoring the status quo of others' expectations was my normal. This much is certain: I wasn't at home in my own skin. And I don't want to live that way.

A break in our normal routines offers us a profound gift: an opportunity for reassessment, renewal, and replenishment, to embrace change and give space to our best selves. But will I decline the gift and "return" to my addictions of hurry, obsession, distraction, fueling my temptation to get ahead, leaving no empty space? Where there is empty space, it's illuminating to see what is exposed.

Writing from the madness of the Holocaust, Victor Frankl reminded us that we don't get to choose our difficulties, but we do have the freedom to select our responses.

Today, here's the life I choose.

One. There's an Irish proverb that reads, *Ar scáth a chéile a mhair-imíd;* "In the shadow of each other we live." This wisdom is indispensable. This is about we, not me. Today, let's change our questions. In the shadow of one another, what can I do to make a safe place for you, where the fruit of the Spirit can grow? Can you think of someone for whom that is true or someone who, during this time, feels left out of that shadow (where the inequality is profoundly real)? Please reach out.

Two. Who we are now is enough, if only we have eyes to see. Or, perhaps, we can surrender expectations that, in the end, prevent us from seeing. Such as anticipated lottery winnings, I suppose, with the promise that life can be found "if only," or "when we return to normal." We recognize that freedom happens only when we can let go.

And the gifts born in grace? Vulnerability, empathy, inclusion, compassion, presence, and authenticity.

When I let go of that script, I can let myself be arrested by beauty. Lee Jastor (a friend and Episcopal priest) went into his garden to pray. The fragrance undid him. He was smitten by an Asiatic lily, intoxicating, mesmerizing. He spent the next twenty minutes giddy as a kid, he told me. "I was so undone," he lamented, "I forgot to pray."

"And I felt chastised and guilty. Until it hit me. Being undone by the lily, and savoring its beauty was my prayer." Meister Eckhart is often quoted as saying, "There is a huge silence inside each of us that beckons us into itself, and the recovery of our own silence can begin to teach us the language of heaven."

Mizuta Masahide (seventeenth-century Japanese poet and samurai) spoke a truth that does my heart good, "Barn burned down. Now I can see the moon."

Spirituality and growth begin here. In this moment. I am not a pawn or victim or puppet. I can embrace the sacrament of the present moment, in this conversation, this conundrum, this moment of grace, this relationship, this quarantined day. It could be why Jesus rocked the status quo when he told everyone that the kingdom of heaven is within. Now.

Three. We can let our light spill, as healers, peacemakers, and restorers. Let us heal with our words, with kindheartedness. And here's the deal: To spill light, we don't even have to be good at it. This isn't a contest. Or a test. It's just something we're made for.

I receive email from people unsettled, tired, and scared, looking for words. "Are we going to be OK? How do we pause internally to find refuge? Relief? Sanctuary?"

I close my eyes and vividly remember the times in my life when the fragile nature of my world felt like a breaking point. And I want more than anything to give them a reassuring and consummate answer. And I laugh at my own performance constraint, now wondering which anxiety is gloomier.

For anyone unsettled, I give them a bit of wisdom from the Natal tribes in South Africa. They greet one another each day, saying "*Sawabona*," which means literally, "I see you." The response is "*Sikhona*," which means "I am here." Yes.

When standing knee-deep in the uncertain, it's so easy to be derailed by tensions from the "unknown," as if we can only "move forward" with some kind of resolution or tidiness. But what if I allow tensions to expand my heart and invite me to new appreciation of the sufficiency that is already there, inside? And from that, I embrace the capacity to create a community of kindred spirits kindling the courage we need to show up, even in a messy world?

There's something alluring about filling any empty space. And besides, I'm good at it. This is all the more palpable when we stare at empty days and we're not so sure what to do with them. And there is something very unnerving about being asked to empty (or let go of) whatever I've stockpiled to fill that space. But when there is no empty space, we pay the price. We are full. Stuffed. Numb. Literally numb. When my senses are numbed by noise and overload and worry, I am impoverished.

Bottom line, I become (in the words of Leonardo Da Vinci) a man who "looks without seeing, listens without hearing, touches without feeling, eats without tasting, moves without physical awareness, inhales without awareness of odor or fragrance, and talks without thinking."

"Ultimately, we have just one moral duty," Etty Hillesum wrote. "To reclaim large areas of peace in ourselves, more and more peace, and to reflect it toward others. And the more peace there is in us, the more peace there will also be in our troubled world."

Yes. That's the gift.

The space enables me to see the sufficiency that is already there.

The space enables me to be at peace with my enoughness.

The space enables me to know that my enoughness is never predicated on what I've collected (or on anything external), but on the gentle hands of grace that hold me no matter what.

And, as Etty wrote, this kind of peace spills to the world around us.

At the end of his life, Beethoven wrote his Ninth Symphony. I can only imagine that he wished for (prayed for) other circumstances. He was deaf. He was driven to melancholy. Yes, he wished for relief. And yet, from that place he wrote the Ninth with its soaring "Ode to Joy." I love this story because it is about that internal switch. Beethoven celebrated the beauty that was within. He added voices, turning symphony into opera. And he invites us to engage with the music and beauty inside ("large areas of peace in ourselves"), and to share our own song.

In every single one of us, the music is alive and well. Maybe not the Ninth Symphony, fair enough. Even so, play it. Sing it. Live it. Don't worry whether it's a good enough song or if you have the words right, or that you didn't hear the song earlier. Savor the music. Here's the good news: When I'm at home in my own skin, I can be on the lookout for those who are derailed and cannot hear the music in their world.

Chapter Nine

Stories without Endings

Our world is on tilt. I don't think we have any argument there. And for some, it feels harder to navigate (for our heart or spirit) when we don't feel like we have a script (the stabilizing effect of resolution). It is no surprise that fatigue is real. And many people are just hanging on (financially or emotionally or both). For real. Not from inconvenience, but real pain, real loneliness, real sickness, and real death to people they love. And it never helps when there are cracks in our human connections.

—May 11, 2020

I prefer my life and my stories with cloudless endings. Can you relate? You know, stories with a beginning, a middle, and an end tied up neatly with twine and sealed with a kiss. The ones we tell with great satisfaction, lessons drawn out like fresh honey from the hive.

But the truth is that most stories are larger, and we are invited to make our homes right amid the mystery. And when things don't fit, it can trigger exasperation ("I didn't sign up for this"). And in our spirit, there is a blinking light, reminding us that our emotional fuel level is low.

On my walk, I ask the sheep about stories without endings. That doesn't seem to register. So I ask, "You guys have this thing—living the present—down, with no anxiety. What's up with that?"

The answer came in their unruffled demeanor, "It helps to distinguish between big world and small world."

That does my heart good. Yes. Too often, with "big world" (especially looking for that cloudless day), the news feels unnerving, in your face, and stoked with anger. No wonder we feel as if our control is demoted. No wonder we ask, how can I make a difference in this broken world if the story is still befuddling and unfolding? That's just it: We make a difference in the "small world."

The small world is the place where we stand. Today. With questions, inconvenience, pain, messy stories, and all.

The small world is where we care, where we give a damn. Where we hug (even virtually) and give and try and love and fall down and get up and repent and cry and embrace and challenge and reconcile and heal. And make sure we tell those not doing so good, "We've got you." The small world that we touch and begin to heal.

Here's the deal: Now, we can live out the story—our story—with new self-compassionate eyes.

We live grounded in sufficiency and grace. Before we arrive or solve, we can simply be. Instead of seeking to abruptly pass through a threshold, we can pause. And in so doing, we learn, and know what we now carry. John Philip Newell reminds us:

> Do we know that within each one of us is the unspeakably beautiful beat of the Sacred? Do we know that we can honor that Sacredness in one another and in everything that has being? And do we know that this combination—growing in awareness that we are bearers of Presence, along with a faithful commitment to honor that Presence in one another and in the earth—holds the key to transformation in our world?"

We spill this light using "small world" skills. Small world, the world we touch. Skills like compassion, empathy, understanding, and recognition of the other. The very skills that change lives, one heart and one mind at a time.

Have you ever had a conversation with someone and used the same words, but they didn't mean the same things, giving *flabbergast* a new significance? I'm learning that fatigue easily gives way to anger or wallowing or resentment or umbrage. And I don't need that. They are corrosive. And that never turns out well.

How do we measure what matters? Without expecting to be graded? And who gets to choose?

Of course, I needed to ask my quarantine congregation, the sheep. I think I humor them. I hope I do. I can be quite funny, I've been told. I tell them a joke. They don't laugh. So, I'm betting they think I'm a poet.

"I need your help. Last Sunday, in our church readings, we read about you. Psalm 23. It was about being led to green pastures and quiet waters."

"You humans complicate things, don't you?" their looks told me.

And I smile. And it hits me. Green pastures and quiet waters aren't about a Hallmark card moment, are they? This is more fundamental and pragmatic. This is about sustenance. Replenishment. The sacrament of the present moment. And it refreshes the soul.

Where are my green pastures and quiet waters?

One. Our well-being comes from the inside. You are a child of God, and it wouldn't hurt to cut yourself some slack. Self-compassion grounds us.

Two. There is healing in beauty: the sacred in the ordinary of our everyday. This changes my first question to anyone, "What did you savor today?" And this is important: savoring beauty, the sacred in the ordinary, doesn't ask for closure or resolution.

Some time back, a friend had the courage to tell me that his life was on the brink, and he held himself back, not thinking he would be allowed into a life (or world) of abundance and permission and joy and grace. He didn't ask for my advice, and I didn't really have any, but I wanted to write him anyway.

> I was thinking about your comments—re: being excessively fragile and vulnerable—thinking that I didn't know what to say, sipping my Dow's Port while watching Monday Night Football, and remembering the times in my life when I felt on the edge or in some way susceptible to shattering (both shattered, and shattering someone, anyone around me), and trying to remember what triggered those times, and I came up with zero. If all else fails, I'd be more than happy to pour you a glass of port and offer you a chair on the back deck to watch the sun set over Puget Sound, and hope for a little luck that maybe we'd see a bald eagle float by, and tell you that I don't know much, "but that sure is a damn fine eagle, isn't it?" Who knows, before the light gives way completely, we could wander over to the garden and take a hit of fragrance from the rose Souvenir de la Malmasion, and marvel at the different ways the universe lets us get intoxicated, loitering in the moment, knowing full well that this drunkenness—like any other—comes with a price: the bittersweet reality that it can never quite fill that pit in our soul, even though it comes close, Or, we can stay put on the deck, crank up the music, let Jackson Browne fill the dark and the empty spaces, swap stories with a good friend, and hope that the angels are taking notes on recommendations for ways to make eternity heavenly.

Three. It's OK to live wholehearted without resolution.

I was raised in a faith that required closure of some kind. So there was no invitation to pause and see and savor, simply for the sake of savoring. But closure isn't the answer. Our heart can hold more than we think. Sadness isn't our enemy. And our hunger for resolution can make us forget to savor the sacrament of the present.

I'm grateful for Pema Chödrön's wisdom from her book *When Things Fall Apart*:

> The only time we ever know what's really going on is when the rug's been pulled out and we can't find anywhere to land. We use these situations either to wake ourselves up or to put ourselves to sleep. Right now—in the very instant of groundlessness—is the seed of taking care of those who need our care and of discovering our goodness.

Spilling good brings clarity, maybe especially in times of uncertainty. Because sometimes, life can feel too big. Too precarious. Times that break us, undo us. Times when the labels we give our limitations make our anxiety or fear feel bigger than life itself. And sometimes (if I'm honest), I've got nothing to give. But I'm a storyteller, and I take consolation in stories about our human capacity for recovery and renewal. When I focus on what is missing, I do not see my capacity for enoughness, inside.

The ordinary moments of every day (even those that confuse us, unnerve us, or break our hearts) are hiding places of the holy. Where the sacred is alive and well. Where hope grows. Anxiety and vulnerability are real, yes. But the answer is not to chase vulnerability away. It's the opposite. My vulnerability is the signal that I am human, with the capacity to be stretched, to give my heart, to be broken, to cry with those who break, to spill good. And I don't ever want to lose that.

Chapter Ten

Finding Strength in One Another

As I write this, many find themselves in the crosshairs of the debate about going back to "church" (meaning back to a building). Thank you, John Pavlovitz, for this: "That's the beautiful truth of these dark days: even in the middle of a terrifying pandemic, even when schedules are interrupted, even when chaos is ever-present, even when people are scattered, even when buildings filled with chairs and pews and class rooms are closed—the Church is still the Church and love is still love."

—*May* 25, 2020

This morning with my congregation, the sheep, I just stood by the fence, and watched, my spirit a bit downcast.

"Are you going to preach," one asked, "or not?"

"Not today," I told them. "I just want to talk, if that's OK. And I need you all to listen."

"Oh, good. That's much better than a sermon."

"I'm thinking about my other 'congregation,'" I tell them. "I travel and speak to groups. But now I can't, and won't be able to for some time."

"Do you miss them?"

"Yes, I do."

Andre Dubus wrote stories about regular people, like bartenders, mechanics, waitresses, and the like. In 1986, after publishing several books of short stories, Dubus stopped to help a couple stranded on the side of the highway, and he was hit by a passing car. Dubus saved the woman's life by throwing her out of the way, but he lost one of his legs and spent the rest of his life in a wheelchair.

He wrote, "Some of my characters now feel more grateful about simple things—breathing, buying groceries, sunlight—because I do."

In *Love in the Time of Cholera*, Gabriel Garcia Marquez wrote that "he allowed himself to be swayed by his conviction that human beings are not born once and for all on the day their mothers give birth to them, but that life obliges them over and over again to give birth to themselves."

What a gift. And here's the deal: Rebirth is not just for getting my act together or punching a ticket for eternity, but a reclamation of a part of me that has been buried or lost or forgotten.

There is no doubt that we are living in a time of rebirth, when life invites us (maybe even obliges us) to give birth to ourselves again. With all due respect to the church of my youth, I have been born again and again and again, and each time, I have found a life and a world to love with all my heart.

Because there are times when I forget. That the light—of compassion and empathy and kindheartedness and gratitude (humanity)—spills from ordinary lives, in ordinary moments, one gesture at a time. One moment of wonder at a time. One moment of being fully alive, fully awake, fully present, at a time. (And yes, even in moments tainted by crisis and tragedy, as each ordinary moment is the hiding place for the holy.)

Yes. That's another thing we forget: that every day of our lives we are walking sermons in gestures small and heartfelt. That we, in this new and awkward and frustrating and enlivening dance of needing and wanting and caring without the capacity to touch, find the compassionate love of Jesus incarnated in our work and our words. In cards and letters and Zoom connections. In artistic creations and phone calls and meals delivered to those who are without. In errands run and masks made and prayers lifted. Each single gesture, a portal to grace with power precisely because of our bigger world uncertainty.

In rebirth, we draw from the well of compassion. Beginning with self-compassion.

We wake up to:

- a new core to our own spiritual life,
- a new sense of gratitude,
- a new affirmation of stillness and silence and prayer,
- a new appreciation for relationships and community,
- a new sensitivity to the vulnerable and the needy,
- a new understanding of our own capacity and enoughness,
- a new realization that our God has always been too small.

This is not easy. Birth never is. But "Compassion asks us to go where it hurts," Henri Nouwen writes, "to enter into places of pain, to share in brokenness, fear, confusion, and anguish. Compassion challenges us to cry out with those in misery, to mourn with those who are lonely, to weep with those in tears. Compassion requires us to be weak with the weak, vulnerable with the vulnerable, and powerless with the powerless. Compassion means full immersion in the condition of being human."

When life turns left, we can:

- Fight it. Pretend it isn't real. Feel hemmed in and cornered, so there has to be an enemy. We name them. And we draft God to fight on our team. This choice is never good for the blood pressure.
- Feed it. Fan the flame with worry and fretfulness, finding solace in Armageddon. This one also needs an enemy and blood pressure medicine.
- Numb it. Numb it with you name it, anything in order to not feel, or see.

Or, we can sit with it a spell. We can listen, notice, pay attention, learn. We can make space for vulnerability and precariousness and grace and humility. We can lay down what encumbers us (anger, restlessness, and so on). And we can invite rebirth.

Chapter Eleven

Nothing Small about Compassion

I think I know why the death toll doesn't compute with so many, because we can't connect to their narratives. Only when there is a name does it feel real. So, what do we do? I was schooled to know what to say. The "right" words, mostly for appearance. As if what I had to say was more important than that I'm here. And I forget the power of simply being present. A witness. One person at a time. A bestower of grace and light in a dark world.

—*May 31, 2020*

On my walk this morning, I stop, and stand at the fence. My congregation, the sheep, doesn't mind silence, which is nice and different from many churches I have visited.

After a while, I tell them, "I need your help. My heart hurts today, and I don't know what to say. Or do. I know you all don't read the news. But the world is broken. It's been an exhausting and terrible week." They look up at me.

"You don't mind if I stand here a little while, do you?" I ask. "It's peaceful here."

And I tell them about the 106,000 people who have died from COVID-19. And about George Floyd, killed by police, pleading for his life with the words, "I can't breathe," and how he called out for his mother in his final moments.

"Today there are riots in cities, with fires," I tell them, "which is striking because today is Pentecost Sunday, which is about the fire of the Holy Spirit. I feel like I'm rambling. I'm sorry."

"You sure do apologize a lot," their look tells me.

"Well, I grew up in a church that always required answers. And I don't have any," I tell them. "But I can tell you a story."

> A young girl returns home from school in tears. Her mother, worried, asked, "Sweetheart, what happened?"
>
> "It was awful," the girl told her mother. "My best friend's cat died. And she was very, very sad. And I don't think I'm a good best friend, because I didn't know the right words to say, to try to help her."
>
> "What did you do?" the mother asked.
>
> "I just held her hand and cried with her all day."

"Thank you," I tell my congregation. "You did my heart good today. You helped me remember what matters."

I tell them what Mother Teresa said, "If we have no peace, it is because we have forgotten that we belong to each other." I think they liked it.

The West Wing has always been one of my TV comfort foods. I don't know how many times I've watched the series. But it never gets old. It's even better with dark chocolate and a glass of wine.

In one episode, Toby Ziegler, White House communications director, is called to the National Mall (the land between the Lincoln Memorial and the U.S. Capitol), because his business card is found in the coat of a homeless man who has died of exposure from extreme cold. The explanation is simple. Toby had given his coat to Goodwill.

But the experience affects Toby deeply. From a tattoo he had seen on the man's arm, he knew the man to be a veteran. Back in his office he calls Veterans Affairs, with hope of figuring out the man's story, or at least finding his next of kin. There is no luck.

> Mandy (White House media consultant) walks into Toby's office while he is on another long hold. "What's going on?"
>
> "A homeless Korean War Vet died of exposure out on the mall last night. I don't know if his family has been contacted. I don't know...what kind of burial..." He trails off, clearly frustrated.
>
> "How do you know him?" Mandy asks.
>
> "I don't."
>
> "Then what does it matter to you?"

This made my heart stop.

There is nothing small about compassion. There is nothing small about making a difference in the life of one human being. But sometimes, we need an experience like Toby's to rock our world. Or, to invite us to hit the reset button. You know, back to what makes us human. To say yes to whatever connects us, as humans, as children of God, as people who need compassion and mercy for sustenance, as people who cannot walk this journey alone. And to say no to whatever divides or demeans or belittles or degrades or incites hate and exclusion. And I must speak that yes, and speak that no, not only with my voice, but with my hands and my feet. Lord hear my prayer.

When the world feels small and dark and frightful, it is not surprising we choose to protect our hearts. We do not easily give them away. This happens when we live from the notion that we carry only so much emotional capital—you know, that precious commodity which allows us to pay attention, to focus, to contribute, to care, to forgive, to set free. So, it goes without saying that conservation is called for. And it becomes our default. "There is no need to spend empathy on just anybody," we think. "We need to pick and choose." Or more bluntly, "There are those who deserve care, and those who don't."

Lord, help us. We lose track of the values that sustain us.

There is nothing small about compassion. It is the thread of life woven through each day. As humans—in the image of God—we touch, love, give, receive, and redeem. It's time to rethink our notion about the scarcity of compassion.

This is an affirmation of what is already alive and well within each of us. We have the capacity to be places of shelter and hope and inclusion and healing.

Chapter Twelve

Some Stories Are Too Heavy to Carry Alone

This was another hard week for me. The news, yes. And many conversations (phone and email) about our world (and our place in it), and how it is easy to feel, or to be, quite literally, lost. And lost is not just a GPS malfunction. Too many know what it means to be disconnected, discounted, diminished, demeaned. Lost.

—June 8, 2020

On my walk this morning, I stop at the fence. My congregation is reclining contentedly in the grass. "Well," their look asked me. "Do you have a story this week or not?"

"It's an old story," I tell them. "It's about a lost sheep." And that seemed to perk them up. (But then, we preachers always see what we want to see.)

"This shepherd had one hundred sheep. And one of them was lost."

I stood silent a little while, wondering if the story would make them uncomfortable. "And the shepherd leaves the ninety-nine sheep to go out and find the lost one. He brings him home."

In the story, the shepherd doesn't blame the lost one. Or give advice. Or admonish. Because to the shepherd, that sheep is not just a number, but a face, a name and a story. The shepherd knew that some stories are too heavy to carry alone. That every one of us at some time in our life will need the loving arms of justice, mercy, and unmerited grace. Some days we are the lost. And some days, we are the hands and feet of the shepherd.

My good friend Ed Kilbourne wrote a song called "Promised Land." I can't carry a tune, so I read it to the sheep. They didn't seem to mind.

> There's a place they call the promised land where people
> live by grace
> The leaders are their servants, the last ones win the race
> And those who love are wealthy and those who hate are poor
> And honor's won by making peace, not by making war
> And everyone's invited when the kingdom feast is spread
> They remember how they got there in the breaking of the bread
> They pass a cup around the room to every tear stained face
> And drink a toast to Jesus as they sing Amazing Grace.

Some days we are the one lost. And some days, we are the hands and feet of the shepherd. Because some stories are too heavy to carry alone. As a young pastor, I would ask people to be involved with certain ministries—many having to do with real-life trauma, supporting people and finding a place for healing and community and redemption. It's messy work. And many, who found healing in these gatherings themselves, would answer, "I'd love to be involved, but I'm sorry, I can't. I'm not even remotely qualified."

And my answer, "Good, then, you're perfect for the job."

Skill sets are one thing. We can teach them. And procedures and protocols can be learned (and in too many cases in church, they can be happily unlearned). But a whole heart, an honest awareness, and an admission of what it means to be a lost sheep, to know sorrow in your heart, and a willingness to set down the moniker of expert and to say, "Please let me carry you" is enough.

It's easy to be unnerved by it all. For starters, this story would make more sense if it had a wolf. Find an enemy and channel the energy of domination and the tactics of war. No wonder the tsunami of information distracts and overwhelms. And I react (taking sides before I try to listen and understand). The tsunami wins. It drowns my voice, which means I can't hear the good news; the truth that I still have a role to play.

We're afraid to let "try" be our first step. And we're afraid to let "fail" be our second step. And because of that, we never see the joy of finding lost sheep and carrying them home.

On a Saturday morning in 2013, I stood in the kitchen of the Dexter Avenue Baptist Church Parsonage, the home to the Rev. Dr. Martin Luther King Jr. and his family from 1954 to 1960. It reminded me of a story he told in one of his sermons. By the time the Montgomery bus strike was achieving both success and national attention, Dr. King began receiving telephone death threats (as many as forty a day). Here's the story as I recall it:

> One night very late around midnight—and you can have some strange experiences at midnight—the telephone rang. On the other end was an ugly voice.
>
> For some reason, it got to me. I was weak. Sometimes, I feel discouraged. You can't call on Daddy anymore. You could only call on the Something your Daddy told you about, that Power that can make a way out of no way.
>
> I prayed. "Lord, I'm down here trying to do what's right. But I must confess, I'm losing my courage."
>
> I could hear an inner voice saying to me, "Martin Luther, stand up for truth. Stand up for justice. Stand up for righteousness."

I stood by that kitchen table where Martin Luther King prayed in the middle of the night and something clicked for me. When I see acts of courage I see heroism, but I don't see myself. Instead, I see how far I have to go. Or I see how far short I have fallen. But I do understand tired. And I do understand discouraged. And I do understand the end of my resources.

Thank you, Dr. King, for the reminder. I do understand that some stories are too heavy to carry alone. That some days we are the one lost. And some days, we are the hands and feet of the shepherd.

The Talmud reminds us, "Do not be daunted by the enormity of the world's grief. Do justly now, love mercy now, walk humbly now. You are not obligated to complete the work, but neither are you free to abandon it."

Chapter Thirteen

I Am Because We Are

I'm watching the ways we all carry pain, in a week where the news can leave us feeling heartbroken, helpless, fearful, enraged, or disgusted. Or, just dizzy. And it doesn't help if I see pain only as my enemy or source of shame.

—June 15, 2020

"I've told a lot of people about you all," I tell the sheep this morning on my walk. And I tell them the story of the young woman with hives.

A young woman with a very serious case of hives went to a specialist for relief. She had suffered for some time, living in continual pain because the hives covered much of her body. She needed healing, and hoped that a doctor could prescribe a cure. But his diagnosis surprised her. "There is no medicine I can give you," he told her. "You see, your skin is crying because you cannot."

"He sure talks a lot," I hear one of the young ones say to his momma as I start to leave. "And I don't understand anything that he's saying."

"That's OK," I think I hear her say. "It does his heart good to talk to us. And we're good listeners. That's what matters most to him right now."

Do you know the word *ubuntu*? A Nguni Bantu term meaning "humanity," it is often translated as "I am because we are." In a philosophical sense, it refers to "the belief in a universal bond of sharing that connects all humanity."

As chairman of the South African Truth and Reconciliation Commission, Desmond Tutu used descriptive words to speak about *ubuntu*, intimately binding it within Christian principles of goodness. In his book *No Future Without Forgiveness*, he describes the person true to *ubuntu* as one who is "generous, hospitable, friendly, caring and compassionate." He says it is a state in which one's "humanity is caught up and inextricably bound up" in others. Tutu says of *ubuntu*, "I am human because I belong, I participate, I share."

We have all experienced pain. And it has appeared on the doorstep of our heart in a variety of ways; our life (or our world) takes a left turn, or we find ourselves emotionally overdrawn (literally heart-weary), or for whatever reason, we continue to feel small. From this tug of war, our "hives" can be a metaphor for any number of things that afflict us. But in the end, we run or we shut down because we see our pain and our brokenness as blemishes—our fault line and our shame. Something to hide.

But this I know to be true: Whether it is conflict or sorrow or grief or anxiety or self-pity, I cannot bury pain without mortgaging something else to keep it hidden. Richard Rohr reminds us, "If we do not transform our pain, we will most assuredly transmit it."

An old Cherokee is teaching his grandson about life. "A fight is going on inside me," he tells the boy. "It is a relentless fight that takes a toll, and it is between two wolves. One wolf is evil — he is rage, envy, sorrow, regret, greed, arrogance, self-pity, guilt, resentment, inferiority, lies, false pride, superiority, and ego."

He continues, "The other wolf is good — he is joy, peace, love, hope, serenity, humility, kindness, benevolence, empathy, generosity, truth, compassion, and faith. And this same fight is going on inside you, and inside every other person, too."

The grandson thinks about what his grandfather tells him for a minute and then asks, "Which wolf will win?"

The old Cherokee replies, "The one you feed the most."

Yes, there are parts of ourselves that we do not like, or do not understand, or avoid, or bury. There's nothing new about that. Except that we fuel the fire with an assumption that our priority is to fix the problem. Or at the very least, to look good trying. Sometimes we hide. Sometimes we pretend. Sometimes we get busy being helpful to others.

Sometimes we go to a specialist for advice. I have nothing against specialists. (I've spent a fair amount of money on a few.) It's just that when we believe the solution is disease-removal, we tinker and trade one infomercial or Bible verse or well-intentioned guru for another, believing that there is beauty only after the fix.

I know the fight to be impervious (heart in a fortress and picture-perfect). To be chagrinned by my pain and by my tears. So, I worked so hard at unruffled theology and emotional solutions for that pain, and I unwittingly transmitted it. I missed the beauty. I did not see the power of the gift.

It isn't easy to embrace pain or all that is vulnerable and broken within us. But that is when healing begins. Today, I choose to feed the good (life-giving) wolf. Today, I choose to invite this self, this vulnerable, broken Terry, to the table to speak. This sacrament of the present becomes a place for honesty and confession and learning and empathy and healing. When I do this, I see that we are not on this journey alone.

Chapter Fourteen

On Edge

"Happy Father's Day," I tell the sheep on my walk this morning. In my memory I'm back in southern Michigan, the son of a brick mason. I've been on countless constructions sites. Most of them as a hod carrier (mixing mortar, lugging bricks). So many days eager to quit. And hearing my father's words, "Son, build this one like you're building your own." (Eighteen years ago, my father helped me build the house I am in today, a great Father's Day memory.)

—June 22, 2020

Why do you look tired?" one of the sheep asks me this morning.

"I let my spirit get on edge," I tell them. "There's so much to do. My world is hungry for people to step up and embrace becoming bigger and better, including the discomfort that accompanies it, even if we don't fully understand it yet. To give our hearts to creating a world, even if that is the small world around us, where sanctuary is real, where racism and bigotry stop. A world that embraces the human, vulnerable, broken, passionate, and redemptive self of anyone who crosses our path."

"Did you practice that speech?" their look tells me. "That was pretty good. So, why are you still on edge?"

I smile. "You got any advice?

"Stay emotionally and spiritually hydrated."

"Fair enough."

"And, a little joy and laughter wouldn't hurt. You know it's the superpower of resilience, and it'll boost your immunity. Just because the world is overwhelmed doesn't mean you have to be."

This makes me laugh. "This is why I like talking with you all."

As I'm walking away, I hear one of the little ones say, "And don't forget, more love and more stories wouldn't hurt either."

This is the story that came to mind.

An elderly carpenter is eager to retire. He tells his employer (a very well-respected contractor) of his plans to leave the house-building business. He wishes to live a more leisurely life with his wife and extended family. He knows he will miss the paycheck, but it's time to retire and his family will get by.

"I've hammered enough nails for one lifetime," he tells his employer, with a laugh. There's no need to put myself out any longer, he tells himself.

The contractor is very sorry to see his best carpenter go, and asks, "Would you be willing to oversee the building of just one more house, as a personal favor to me?"

Hesitant, the carpenter says yes. In a short time, it becomes easy to see that his heart is not in his work. He resorts to substandard workmanship and uses inferior materials. It is an unfortunate way to end a dedicated career.

When the carpenter finishes his work, the employer comes to inspect the house. The contractor hands the front door key to the carpenter.

"This is my gift to you," he says. "This is your house."

Most of us have been there. Holding those keys. And it never helps slip-sliding down the if-only stream. We know where that takes us.

We make a difference with every nail we hammer, each board we choose, each brick we mortar, each window we put in place. Because we live in a culture of bluster and ado, we forget that we can make a difference. And more often than not, the wrong people get the attention. I'm with David Orr here, "The plain fact is that the planet does not need more successful people. But it does desperately need more peacemakers, healers, restorers, storytellers, and lovers of every kind." Here's to the restorative power of small gestures, one nail at a time.

We are, all of us, builders. We are about the business of building places and spaces for human dignity and inclusion and justice and hope. For resilience and confidence and courage and safety and well-being. But this is important. This parable is not meant to scold us into making a difference. It's a recognition that we have been created and are able to do so. It's not about bootstraps and willpower and consternation. This is about letting the language of our (replenished and not overwhelmed) heart speak.

When I live from "overwhelmed," I react, I live fear, I give in to cynicism. No wonder the first to go are my courage and my ability to laugh. Which is not good considering that they both come from the same muscle in our heart.

Invited to guest-preach at another parish, Rev. Barbara Brown Taylor asked the priest, "What do you want me to talk about?"

"Come tell us what is saving your life now," he told her.

Taylor writes in *An Altar in the World*, "I did not have to say correct things that were true for everyone. I did not have to use theological language that conformed to the historical teachings of the church. All I had to do was figure out what my life depended on. All I had to do was figure out how I stayed as close to that reality as I could, and then find some way to talk about it that helped my listeners figure out those same things for themselves."

Home (in my own skin), that "safe space to regain my bearings, reclaim my soul, heal my wounds, and return to the world as a wounded healer," Parker Palmer writes in his book *On the Brink of Everything: Grace, Gravity, and Getting Old*. "It's not merely about finding shelter from the storm—it's about spiritual survival and the capacity to carry on."

Chapter Fifteen

Finding Resilience

"I need your help," I say to my congregation, the sheep, this morning. "Why does it look so easy for you to live so fully in the present moment?"

My question is met with blank stares and chewing.

Finally, a little one speaks, "We didn't know there was any other option."

—June 29, 2020

I didn't want to tell him that we humans go out of our way to manufacture all kinds of options, to make life more complicated. The result? A Hopi word *koyaanisqatsi*. It translates to "life out of balance." Of course it doesn't take a long, unfamiliar word to know the problem. But it helps to know that it's been around a while. Life's difficulties and obligations impact us all. They pinch, constrain, and put blinders on us. So, it's not that we don't pay attention; it's just that, with our blinders, we may not even notice.

And let's be honest, the present moment may not always be to our liking. It's no wonder we want to rearrange or tidy up. So, we make living in the present a skill set to acquire, and an item for our to-do list. In other words, we will figure it out one of these days.

We miss the invitation of intimacy with the present, the invitation of our tender and humble and whole self, with our capacity to find grace and to savor and to embrace and to care and to invest. To make a difference. To be here now.

I remember a haunting little memoir entitled *The Diving Bell and the Butterfly*, the story of Jean-Dominique Bauby, former editor of the French fashion magazine *Elle*. At the age of forty-three, Jean-Dominique suffered a rare kind of stroke in his brain stem. He woke after twenty days in a coma. Only his left eye functioned. But his mind was unimpaired. He was frozen in a body that had but one meager way to communicate.

It's the story about what it is like to be locked up, a prisoner in your own skin. I cannot imagine the terror, the claustrophobia. It is one thing to feel misunderstood; it is quite another to have utterly no recourse. To feel completely at the mercy of your body, medical advice, random opinions from others, the good will of friends and acquaintances, and above all else, silence. In this case, the indictment of silence.

It was in that world that Bauby learned to probe inlets of sanity, or as he called them, the "only window to my cell." To fall prey to daydreams of walking and talking. To find the "hours drag on but the months flash by." And then this:

> Far from such din, when blessed silence returns, I can listen to the butterflies that flitter inside my head. To hear them, one must be calm and pay close attention, for their wingbeats are barely audible. Loud breathing is enough to drown them out. This is astonishing: my hearing does not improve, yet I hear them better and better. I must have butterfly hearing.

This story does my heart good. It is a story about finding and embracing the sacrament of the present. A story about resiliency. And ultimately, about love. Love of life, and love of the self I bring to this life.

This all sounds good on paper, but it is not an easy sell, especially when we live in a world where we are fueled by the promise of that imaginary day when all will be easier, or at least back to "normal."

Are we there yet? Are we done now?

Resilience is what happens when we give up control and are willing to embrace the ambiguity. And in that ambiguity, to hear—and to take delight in—the wingbeats of butterflies. To be here now.

Let us remember that, regardless of our circumstances, life pulls us inexorably toward love and beauty, even though they may be wrapped in aching pain and or delicious hope. To engage this pull, this fuel that feeds life, is the sacred necessity of resilience. Which means that resilience allows us to live with intention. Now. We do not put off until tomorrow what can be embraced, enjoyed, felt, or experienced today. This includes our sadness, our disappointment, and our grief.

Where does one get resilience? Or butterfly hearing? Is this a gene only given to the lucky?

Here's the deal: We are not outrunning life. Or outrunning the bad parts of life. Resilience involves inviting all of life in...the longing, hunger, vulnerability, wildness, energy, uncertainty, appetite, hope, humor, beauty, and irony. Only when we embrace do we see. Only when we embrace do we hear with butterfly hearing.

I'm reminded of an article I clipped with a photo of a man giving a testimonial: "It made me feel like a human being again." Is he referring to a church? To a mandatory therapy group? To a motivational seminar? To a *New York Times* bestselling book? No.

He is a former inmate in San Francisco County Jail. Now he is working with the San Francisco Garden Project. He is talking about feeling human again because of his work in a garden.

The Garden Project is a program started for the jail by Cathrine Sneed. In an eight-acre garden, prisoners grow vegetables, and the organic produce is delivered to projects that supply food to seniors, homeless people, and AIDS patients. Above all, the organic, chemical-free garden is a living metaphor for the healthy lives the jail gardeners are trying to create.

Go figure. We go to great lengths (not to mention pay good money) to find balance, to name solutions for our emotional conundrums. The former inmate profiled in this article found the answer when he put his hands in the soil, planted a seed, and watched it grow.

Life pulls us inexorably toward love and beauty. And we find replenishment and balance in places of sanctuary. In sanctuary we do not close life off, we let life in…every bit of life, wholeheartedly, whether that is grief or sadness or bewilderment or gladness or joy. Yes, we can be here now.

"I talk to people about you, just so you know," I tell my congregation, the sheep. "I tell them that you all are the picture of serenity and contentment."

There is no affect in their faces. And I thought they'd be happy with this. Or at least impressed.

A young one asks, "What's serenity?"

"Being glad to be here. Like resting in gladness."

"What else is there?" his look told me.

I smile, knowing all too well our human proclivity: It's OK to be content, but are we content enough? After all, we might be missing out.

In a world where the news cycle and its uncertainty shake the ground we stand on, there is a great treasure in being present. The great treasure of being glad to be alive. The great treasure of heartfelt joy. To be here. Now. This is good news.

And yet, why the inner unrest? Is it our preoccupation with distraction? It is as if we believe that we live from some kind of deficiency. As if we're not where we "should be," or even wish to be.

And inside, (this is my confession), I rage against:

- my fragile nature and inelegant humanity,
- my inability to savor the very ordinary (and yes, messy) moments,
- my feeling "at the mercy of" circumstances,
- my not "achieving" wholeness (like it's a game to win).

This isn't new. Several hundred years ago, Blaise Pascal wrote, "By means of a diversion we can avoid our own company twenty-four hours a day."

But it's not just diversion. It's a kind of itch. A relentless hankering, and pursuit of something always elusive. As if life is always just beyond where we are *now*. I'm all for living the present moment. Just not this one. And yet, the great treasure of a fulfilled life is in the ground where I stand (and walk, work, live, and love).

I tell the sheep that my garden is my teacher. There I find treasures, moments of serenity (resting in gladness), when snapshots, vistas, colors, fragrance make the world stand still. My urgency fades. This is the value in making rituals (containers where we are available to grace).

Here's the paradigm shift: With our cognitive or cerebral approach, we still see the treasure (of being present) as something to acquire. And, we miss that it is alive and well, inside us. There is sufficiency even when the well feels dry. When we see only scarcity, we let anger or blame have its way.

Today, I thank God for butterfly hearing, and for the grace that allows me to risk loving this day.

- To be unafraid of a life that can be messy.
- To make a space for something less than perfect in myself and in those around me.
- To offer kindness or compassion in a glance. In a word. In a touch. In a gesture.
- To create sanctuary spaces where healing and hope are offered; where hatred is turned away.
- To believe in goodness after harm.
- And to know that this love will always spill to the world around me.

Chapter Sixteen

They Are All Our Children

"You guys make me smile," I tell the sheep this morning. "Thank you. I don't feel like I need to prove anything. You all are a sanctuary for me."

They give me that look that tells me they have no idea what I'm talking about. But they don't interrupt, and they give me the space, which is what really matters.

—July 27, 2020

I tell the sheep a story about a reporter covering the fighting and violence during a war in Sarajevo. He watched as a little girl was fatally shot by a sniper. The reporter threw down whatever he held, rushing immediately to the aid of a man who knelt on the pavement cradling the child.

As the man carried the child, the reporter guided them to his car and sped off to a hospital.

"Hurry, my friend." the man urged. "My child is still alive."

A moment or two later he pleaded, "Hurry, my friend. My child is still breathing."

And a little later, "Please, my friend...my child is still warm."

Although the reporter drove as fast as possible, by the time they arrived at the hospital, the little girl had died. As the two men were in the lavatory, washing the blood off their hands and their clothes, the man turned to the reporter and said, "This is a terrible task for me. I must now go tell her father that his child is dead. He will be heartbroken."

The reporter stood speechless. He looked at the grieving man and said, "I thought she was your child."

The man shook his head. "No. But aren't they all our children?"

Yes. They are all our children.

Like any good homilist, I pause, just to let that last line sink in. Not because we don't know it to be true, but when our world is spinning, we easily lose track of the very things that anchor our soul. And in that pause, I remember. I'm not just the preacher. I'm also the child.

That we live in a world unnerving and unpredictable is no revelation. But what always hits me in my gut is our capacity to be cruel and merciless. I know, this is not new. But for some reason, it still disheartens.

And there is a heap plenty to blame—people and systems. (Of course, it is always "other" people, and "other" systems.) But the truth is straightforward. We wound one another. We wound with real wars, and with real bullets. We wound with words, with hatred and resentment and umbrage. And we wound with intolerance and small-mindedness (some of it in the name of God and "love").

"If we have no peace," Mother Teresa reminded us, "it is because we have forgotten that we belong to each other." Well, if we do belong to one another, then "they"—the "least of these" and all those without voices—are indeed, our children. Ours to care for. Ours to listen to. Ours to see.

"Because we have forgotten" is not about some shortcoming in my psyche (something I need to berate myself for, and nurse guilt about). It is an invitation: to remember that the child, cradled in the man's arms, embodies every single one of us. No, we've not fallen victim to a sniper's bullet. But life has rough edges—much, much rougher for many. Especially now.

This, however, is assuredly true: There has been a time in each of our lives when we needed someone to say, "Aren't they all our children?"

When we knew that someone had the interest—the magnitude, the worth, the belovedness—of that child (in us) foremost in mind. And it made a difference in the choices they made. And it made a difference in the choices we make.

Let me pause again. When I read stories about child abuse, or violence to children, I clutch my heart—literally—and here is my confession: I want to go out and hurt someone, anyone who has done these things. And then I read stories about children who have been wounded and who have been abused, and who have found a way to survive. And not only to survive, but to thrive. And to become beacons of hope for us all.

Back to the story: Our prayer is not just about the child's life we're trying to save, but the very freedom to be a child. And to savor the reminder of the light that burns inside every single one of us. The *Imago Dei*—"This little light of mine, I'm gonna let it shine."

Like it or not, our childhood stays with us forever, regardless of our age. And I hope that we do, at times, continue to behave like children. Jesus seemed to think it was a good thing—something about entering the kingdom of heaven and all that.

Childlike behavior may even help one stay pure in heart and to live life simply. Simplicity is always a wonderful thing. And it just may be that we're not childlike enough.

Carl Jung called it the "Divine Child" and Emmet Fox called it the "Wonder Child." Some psychotherapists call it the "True Self," Charles Whitfield called it the "Child Within," and someone later coined the phrase "the Inner Child." Whatever name you use, it refers to that part of each of us that is ultimately alive. It is where our feelings come to life. When we experience joy, sadness, anger, fear, or affection, that child within us is coming to life. Not in order to be measured or to impress, but simply to embrace and to be embraced. To breathe

the holy air of the present moment, in laughter, wonder, openheartedness and unabashed baltering (to balter is to dance without particular skill or grace, but with extreme joy).

Is it possible that we don't trust our own goodness?

"Do not be dismayed by the brokenness of the world. All things break. And all things can be mended. Not with time, as they say, but with intention," L.R. Knost reminds us. "So, go. Love intentionally, extravagantly, unconditionally. The broken world waits in darkness for the light that is you."

What does it mean to embrace the gifts of this child? To embrace the gifts of the child within you?

Sometimes we need to be carried. Sometimes we need to carry. The smallest of words can make the biggest difference. You can be the voice for those who don't have one. "Sometimes our light goes out, but is blown again into instant flame by an encounter with another human being," Dr. Albert Schweitzer wrote, "Each of us owes the deepest thanks to those who have rekindled this inner light."

Chapter Seventeen

Sleeping in the Storm

It's very close to triple digits here today. I know that it's the same for many of you. But here in the Pacific Northwest, we don't know what to do in that kind of heat. Even the sheep gave me the look today, "There will be no church. Because we're not moving." Fair enough. I was tempted to get a sprinkler for them to run through. I'll be doing that later today.

—August 17, 2020

On that day, when evening had come, Jesus said to them, "Let us go across to the other side." And leaving the crowd behind, they took him with them in the boat, just as he was. Other boats were with him. A great windstorm arose, and the waves beat into the boat, so that the boat was already being swamped. But he was in the stern, asleep on the cushion; and they woke him up and said to him, "Teacher, do you not care that we are perishing?" (Mark 4:35-38)

In his book *Have a Little Faith*, Mitch Albom shares this story:

> A young man sought employment on a farm. He handed a letter to his potential employer that read, "He sleeps in a storm." The desperate owner needed help, so he hired the young man despite his enigmatic letter.
>
> Several weeks passed and, in the middle of the night, a powerful storm ripped through the valley. Awakened by the storm, the

> owner jumped out of bed. He called for his new employee, but the man was sound asleep. The owner dashed to the barn and to his amazement, the animals were safe with plenty of food. He hurried to the nearby field only to see that the bales of wheat were already bound and wrapped in tarpaulins. He ran to the silo. The doors were latched and the grain was dry.
>
> And then the owner understood, "He sleeps in a storm."

The storm part—when the world as we know it goes catawampus—we all know. But not all storms are wrapped in weather. Just click on any news source, or for that matter, look in the mirror. Like it or not, none of us is insulated from the common, messy, tragic, inconvenient, and unfortunate experiences of life. And they (the unknown and the weighty) sometimes "strike" so suddenly.

The storm is not just the circumstances (however precarious); the real storm is what recalibrates our internal balance. You know, the storm that keeps us from sleeping. Because we're not our best self.

Our Western mindset world offers plenty of folk peddling all kinds of tonic to escape the vicissitudes of life—a gizmo, or a mantra, or a prayer designed to be some sort of secret handshake with God, or maybe a scented candle to help the mood.

We know this story is not just about a storm; it is about our ability to sleep. Or, more literally, to be at rest. At peace. To, as dancer Katherine Dunham said, "go within every day and find the inner strength so that the world will not blow your candle out." I can tell you, I want some of that. What was the hired hand's secret? I'm asking because I don't easily sleep in a storm. Does anyone?

So here's what happens: When I internalize the storm, I end up living "in between"—meaning I live "as if" or "if only" or "when" (life becomes normal). Which means that I live reactively or at the mercy of (just like the frenetic anxiety of the farmer in the story). Here's the odd part: With our sense of worry, we assume that we are in control. Go figure. And our worry only leaches focus, passion, investment, and energy from all our endeavors.

There is a story about a Zen priest in China when the warlords were plundering villages at the early part of the twentieth century. When this particular village heard that the warlord was headed toward them, all of the people fled to the hills—except one priest. When the warlord arrived, he inquired if anyone was left in the village. The answer was, "Only the priest in the temple." The warlord commanded, "Bring him to me." When the priest was brought into his presence, the warlord drew his sword and cried, "Do you know who I am? I am he who can run you through with this sword and never bat an eye." The Zen priest gave his reply, "Do you know who I am? I am he who can be run through with your sword and never bat an eye."

I want that kind of self-assurance and inner strength to face the threats and storms in my life, don't you? This I know: In the midst of any storm, we survive by affirming who we are. Theologian Paul Tillich, in his book *The Courage to Be*, said that the "ultimate courage is to affirm our being against all the threats of nonbeing." Yes, he is a professor and sounds elegantly academic. Nevertheless, it is also elegantly true. And very good news.

Every day "forces of nonbeing" confront us by saying, "You are nobody, you don't have a right to exist." Or, "This you, is not enough." Or, "When you arrive at such and such, you will find happiness." Or, "Your life will begin after the storm passes." As if our identity and well-being is somewhere outside of us, and that whatever is inside of us is not enough.

No, I'm not advocating that we try to outsmart the storm. Or control it, for that matter. But it does help to remember that it does not control me—or us. And we still have the power, and the choice, to take small steps. Be it "securing the bales," or "latching the silo," let's begin here: If we don't bring it with us, we're not going to find it there. What do I have control over? In other words, what is the one thing I can do?

This much I know: I can begin here. Now. I can offer dollops of kindness to those depleted (including myself). I can stay spiritually hydrated. I can create safe places of inclusion for those wounded and diminished. I can make choices from (and rest in) sufficiency, and not scarcity. I can rest in the truth that my strength (value, fullness, abundance, wholeness) is already alive and well inside, even when I don't see it.

Chapter Eighteen

We Are a Flock

Our sky is blanketed with an eerie gray. For a few days now, it's been a smoke-infused sky. We are told it's from the fires south of us, in Oregon, where tragedy from the fires has reared its head. It is a long way for clouds of smoke to travel. While it is not easy to breathe, it does help us remember and think of those still in harm's way. And to care about our planet, now groaning in pain.

—September 14, 2020

"Do you really talk to the sheep every week?" I was asked this week on a Zoom gathering.

"I do," I tell them. Although truth be told, most days I just stand there and listen. They've got a corner on something that we humans have lost or forgotten. When I pass by this morning, the sheep are all standing, as if waiting for the service to begin. (It makes me feel good to think that's the case.)

"Why are you guys always together?" I ask.

"We're a flock," one little one says.

"We could use that now. We live pretty divided in this world."

Here's what hit me: There are times when we feel at wits' end. There are times when we are certain we cannot handle this. There are times when we feel strong enough to handle everything and wonder why we fail. There are times when the events of our world bewilder and unravel us, even while uniting us in pain. And there are times when our insides feel like dust, when we hope to find something to carry us through. And for too many, one of those times is now.

So I wonder: How do we survive? And where do we go and what do we draw upon when life is bigger than we are? The sheep were right. We must remember that we are a flock. This must be a nonnegotiable: When you hurt, I hurt.

When I think of how my life should be, endurance is not what I had in mind. I have an agenda and a timeline. And it is irritating when life interferes. Or, say, an intersection of calamities: health, economic, racial, democratic, and climatic.

When life is awkward or inconvenient or downright intolerable, we are offered an invitation. Martin Heidegger called it *Dasein* ("being in the world"). This is not a reference to existence, but to our capacity to enter fully into the day. This day. In other words, we are no longer numb. We feel—literally and fully.

What is at stake is not withdrawal or protection or more armor. What is at stake is understanding that spirituality, if anything, is about immersion. A spirituality that begins with the sentence, "I never noticed that before." We find ourselves celebrating (even without knowing it), the sacrament of the present moment. And, if we are lucky, we pass the gift on. And you never know how far that gift will travel.

It is sufficient enough to know that today is a good day to live and to make a difference.

This is a good day…

- To embrace the world like a lover.
- To right a wrong.
- To forgive (beginning with myself).
- To love.
- To embrace.

- To offer a hand, or a kind word. Or both.
- To take a risk.
- To hope. To offer hope.
- To find sanctuary. To offer sanctuary.
- To imagine. To delight.
- To wonder. To wander.
- To sit still. To laugh out loud.
- To question. To dance.
- To drink that bottle of wine (the one that's been saved for a special occasion).
- To savor. To give…and to give again.

And even after reading—and reciting aloud—that list, I need to be honest and tell you that some days I just want to shut down. Or give up. I'm done fighting. And I wonder if I have what it takes.

Chapter Nineteen

Life Stretches Us All

On my walk today, the sheep are resting under a group of fir trees. I stand for a minute and then ask, "What happens when you feel disconnected from your heart?"

"Who wants to know?" one of the little ones asks.

"Oh" I say, "I'm just asking for a friend."

"This week, our world lost another bright light," I tell my congregation. "And my heart hurts. Maybe because this year has been so heavy. To lose such a steadfast pioneer for human rights and gender equality is disheartening to say the least."

—September 21, 2020

Needing a story (with an infusion of hope), my mind gratefully retreats to an unseasonably cool night at Vashon's Red Bike Restaurant. It is packed with patrons for a local fundraiser auctioning creative and bizarrely decorated wellies. Here in the Pacific Northwest, Wellington boots are considered formalwear. I expected good island entertainment. I did not expect to have my heart tugged.

Sporting their wellies, a group of island fourth graders (including my son Zach) brought the house down with a gumboot dance. Fourth graders as storytellers. This is as it should be.

You see, a long time ago, the gumboot dance was born, deep in the gold mines of South Africa. There, under the weight of an unjust and oppressive labor system, workers lived as little more than slaves. Each morning the men were taken in chains down into the mines and shackled at their workstations—facing long, hard, repetitive labor—in almost total darkness. Talking was forbidden.

This is not a story for the faint of heart, for physical abuse was common, and over the years, hundreds of workers were killed in "accidents." Sadly, it continues, in part, to this day.

The floors of the dark mines, with poor or nonexistent drainage, were often flooded, leaving the miners knee-deep in dirty waters, resulting in skin ulcers, foot problems, and consequent lost work time. Instead of draining the mine (costly), the mine owners provided each worker with gumboots (Wellington boots). This created what became the miners uniform, consisting of heavy black Wellington boots, jeans, bare chests (due to the stifling heat), and bandannas to absorb eye-stinging sweat.

Gumboot dancing was born out of adversity, and blood and sweat and tears. Though forbidden to speak, by slapping their gumboots and rattling their ankle chains, the workers sent messages to each other in the darkness, creating a means of connection and communication, essentially their own unique form of Morse code.

Can you imagine what that must have sounded like? In the rattling of chains and the slapping of rubber boots is born the music of hope, the music of angels, the music of freedom, the music of camaraderie and grace.

Their communication evolved into a sort of entertainment, and the miners developed their percussive sounds and movements into a unique song and dance form—sung in Xhosa, Sothu, or Zulu—which they used to entertain one other during their free time. I do not even pretend to comprehend the miners' suffering. However, I can learn from them. Gratefully. Let me rephrase: We all can learn. Especially now.

Yes life stretches us all. Sometimes to the breaking point. Life is difficult, and sometimes, unjust. I have talked about my own battles with anxiety and depression. And I'm grateful for supportive and understanding email messages. Watching fourth graders, I came to the realization that in the midst of uncertainty, it's time to put on your wellies, and do a dance.

"But in a world where we are already stretched, Terry, why write about human suffering?"

Because kindness requires the truth. And the truth is this: Our capacity to give and to care is born in those times we have come face to face with our own vulnerability and intrinsic powerlessness and brokenness. Let us never forget. These are not undesirable traits. No, they reveal the full measure of our humanness and are a testament to a remarkable internal reservoir that includes generosity, courage, and compassion. A reservoir too easily buried.

The gift of the wellies? Our focus changes from our internal noise to the underlying narrative of dignity and internal well-being. The dance is the voice of primary truth. I need this reminder in a world where anger and violence target the vulnerable and the powerless. I may want to turn away. Instead, I am invited to put on my wellies. I am invited to see. And to give, to heal and to dance.

We learn two important lessons from the miners.

One: You never know the impact of a simple gesture. You have no idea the power of compassion and camaraderie that will allow us to not only get through, but to thrive.

Two: In the words of William Kittridge, "We need stories that tell us reasons why...compassion and the humane treatment of our fellows is more important—and interesting—than feathering our own nests as we go on accumulating property and power."

The gumboot dance is about telling a story. To help us remember. It is reminiscent of an Old Testament tradition. When the people of

Israel wandered the desert and began to lose their way or found their morale flagging, they would build a twelve-stone altar, one for each tribe. ("Then Samuel took a stone and set it up between Mizpah and Jeshanah, and named it Ebenezer, for he said, "Thus far the Lord has helped us." [1 Samuel 7:12]) And then, around the altar, they would tell stories.

For the miners, their music became their story. Their source of strength.

I see chains. They hear music.

I see injustice. They see an opportunity to dance.

I see suffering. They see the light of grace.

This is not a matter of positive thinking or denial or extraordinary faith. It is about embracing the sacrament of the present and messy moment.

There is no doubt that we tend to overthink courage. Or compassion. Or resiliency. As if we can create a box or acceptable container. As if it is a task. You know, "tell me what they had, and let's duplicate it." There is no doubt that our circumstances can drown or overwhelm the music.

When we look for what should be, we miss the music in the chaos of what is. When we expect or demand explanation, we miss the miracle that happens in ordinary gumboot dancing.

OK, you want a list?

- Today, tell someone you love them and that they matter.
- Today, share a kind word.
- Today, do a dance, and slap out a message on your wellies.
- Make a difference in someone's life today.

Chapter Twenty

Fear of Missing Out

On my walk, I tell the sheep, "I have a confession. I feel done trying and caring. Life is too mind-numbing. And I'm embarrassed to say so." I stood for a while, waiting for great advice or at least a few ideas on how to get my act together.

They kept grazing, and then one looked up and said, "You just need to know we're glad you're here."

—*September 28, 2020*

It is as if something insidious creeps into our spirit, partly fatigue, or partly something else we cannot name. Regardless, in the end, we believe the messages to be the truth about our life or ourselves. They become our narrative, our script.

"I can't," I will say. "I've got nothing to give."

Who told you that? Does it matter?

In the end, I pull my punches. I quit. Shut down. Give up. Give in to the weight of it all. And something in my spirit or heart hardens. So why even try?

Of course, some of these messages have more stickum than others. Some we lug around for decades from our family of origin. Some messages are internal (we just make them up). Some are odd reinforced prejudices. Even Jesus had to listen to this stuff, "Can anything good come out of Nazareth?" (John 1:46).

But this is not just about building our self-esteem. It is about the reservoir we draw upon in order to live with our whole heart.

But we're only truly stuck if we assume that we have no say in how the story ends. When my heart says, "What's the point?" the narrative of scarcity wins every time. It's not about changing circumstances. It's about embracing what is true and alive and well inside.

"What am I missing?" I ask myself. What am I wanting, yearning for, that I find myself weighted down, or my mind set on pell-mell, hoping to fix it, or find it, or mend it. So, I mentally run and race and call on God, or the sky, or roll the dice with some prayer from my childhood. This will solve it, I tell myself. But the more I push, the more I ask, the more I beseech, the further I move from the center.

Ryoken, a Zen master, lived the simplest kind of life in a little hut at the foot of a mountain. One evening a thief visited the hut, only to discover there was nothing in it to steal. Ryoken returned and caught him in the act. "You may have come a long way to visit me," he told the disillusioned prowler, "and you should not return empty-handed. Please take my clothes as a gift." The thief was bewildered. But he took the clothes and slunk away. Ryoken sat naked, watching the moon, "Poor fellow," he mused. "I wish I could have given him this beautiful moon." Sometimes I feel like that thief. Standing (in my own home, or in front of an audience—well, now on Zoom—or all alone) I am still looking for something, for whatever ails me or creates a hole or emptiness; but, like that thief, not finding it. "What am I missing?" I ask myself. But the more I push, the more I ask, the more I beseech, the further I move from the center.

In my state of distraction, I cannot see that the core of my identity, the place where I stand in this moment (even at times with craziness, and without clarity or stability), I still stand smack-dab in the center of an awesome and illogical grace. Smack-dab in the center of the sacred present.

I forget to give myself the permission to know that I am grounded in the sacred present. I am now able to breathe in and out, and rest in, and live from, this acceptance and grace. And to see in this life, this day, even in the very muddle of the ordinary, even in the very chaos of the ordinary gone awry, the permission to experience a whiff of the holy. God is not waiting until we have it all figured out, or eliminated craziness. The gift of life is in this present moment.

My day may be crazy, but my well-being is not defined only by the craziness (which is real), but by the deep well inside, which holds the gifts of purpose, determination, love, hope, faith, a will to live, joy, and the freedom to help activate healing and redemptive forces in the people who are around me. It works. Every time.

Chapter Twenty-One

Living with a Soft Heart

This morning on my walk, I stop at the pasture fence and stand for a good while. The sheep, lying in the grass, are huddled under a large fir tree. Finally, one asks, "What's up?"

"I have a soft heart. And it bothers me that I've been afraid to say so."

Then I tell them something Pope Francis wrote this week, "Tenderness is the path of choice for the strongest, most courageous men and women." I smile big.

They look at me as if waiting for more.

"That's it for today," I tell them. "Oh, and now, I am no longer afraid of living with a soft heart."

—October 19, 2020

This takes me to a scene in one of my very favorite books, *The Shoes of the Fisherman*. Morris West tells the story of Ukrainian Archbishop Kiril Lakota, who is set free after two decades as a political prisoner in Siberia. Kiril is sent to Rome, where the ailing pope makes him a cardinal. In the novel, the world is in a state of crisis—a famine in China is exacerbated by US restrictions on Chinese trade and the ongoing Chinese-Soviet feud. When the pontiff dies, Lakota—after several ballots—is elected pope. In the book, the new pope, Kiril I, is often plagued by self-doubt, by his years in prison, and by this strange world he knows so little about.

There is one telling conversation, between two of Kiril's advisers.

"What did His Holiness have to say about that?"

"He has a soft heart. The danger is that it may be too soft for the good of the church."

"He has suffered more than we. Perhaps he has more right to trust his heart than we have."

Tenderness is the path of choice for the strongest, most courageous men and women.

And I get it. Really, I do. But if we're honest, this whole soft-heart routine can give us plenty of headaches. Especially in a culture that associates "soft" with weak or frail or compromised or wimpy. It's a strength that hides behind insecurity. And in that kind of world, we see only what we want to see, and we miss the profound truth: the connection between tenderness (soft heart) and courage.

Here's the good news: This is not a project or assignment or test. A tender heart is a gift to embrace. And a gift to spill. A gift that changes the world. When we live from tenderness, we see one another.

When my ego doesn't need to be propped up, I don't need to win any shouting match (which isn't to say shouting doesn't feel cathartic for a wee bit).

Our well-being is grounded in grace. And grace is a voice much bigger than all the other attachments where we may park value or significance. We see that dignity alive in the hearts and souls of those around us. Now, courage takes on a new meaning. Giving us the permission to say yes to choices that invite more soft hearts in a world that needs them.

When we see with our heart, we know that, regardless of our differences, we are on this journey together. A tender heart affirms the inherent value in others, and asks, "What's next?" This is the question the Good Samaritan asked as he stopped for the man in the ditch. Why did he ask it? Because he knew what it was like to be wounded, too.

You see, once we are open to having our stereotypes contradicted, to giving up our expectations and demands, to embracing our brokenness, we begin to see with our wounded heart. When we see with our heart, we are grounded. We are consciously present, no longer numbed. And tender hearts create sanctuaries for those left out. So if ever there was a time for tender-hearted, courageous men and women to step forward, it is now.

Chapter Twenty-Two

Our Core Sufficiency

I spent Saturday morning leading a Zoom retreat (I smile thinking that this was never an aspiration growing up, to lead Zoom retreats. Just sayin'.) I was grateful to spend time with a group, as we talked about embracing the gift of Enough. Which is another way of talking about who or what owns us. And because of Enough, we are not at the mercy of life.

—November 9, 2020

The wind chill this morning hovered in the low thirties, stocking cap and scarf weather, so I tell the sheep that the homily will be brief. That got their attention and I see gratitude in their eyes.

Which reminds me of a story that floated my emotional boat this week.

While a young mother waited at a post-office counter, her four-year-old daughter occupied herself with the opportunity for self-entertainment, exploring around the lobby, looking, prattling, not an item left untouched.

The girl finds a penny on the floor. "Look, Momma," she says proudly, "a penny."

Her mother, busy with a clerk at the window, mumbles an acknowledgment. Others in line smile while some shake their heads and cogitate about the regrettable decline in discipline. The girl walks to the other side of the lobby and places the penny back onto the floor. Feigning surprise, she says, "Look, Momma, I found another penny."

Delighted, she keeps at her enterprise, placing the penny in a different location, until she has found five pennies, each one of them brand-new.

OK. It's a make-you-smile kind of story. Certainly it's meant to lift the spirits, but I'll bet you serious money that I would have likely been one of the curmudgeons. There is nothing like being made to wait in line, sidetracked by a bothersome, disconcerting, and merry child.

And yet, Jesus goes out of his way to connect the kingdom of God with children, and the child within each and every one of us. It is not hyperbole. Because "children live in a world of imagination, a world of aliveness," Mike Yaconelli writes. "Playing Superman and feeling alive, [the child in us] hears a voice deep inside, a warm and loving voice, a living, believing voice, a wild and dangerous voice."

And then somewhere, somewhere along the way, we "grow up," or are tempted by an obligation to "control" life. We realize that we can't fly after all, and our "God-hearing," goes on the blink. We go from flying-wonder-child, to exasperated and intolerant consumer, undone by all the ways we can feel annoyed. Somehow, the gift of just being me isn't enough. And we disconnect from delight and wonder and joy and gratitude. It's as if we lose our true identity.

And here's the good news: When we do lose our way, our authentic self has not vanished. It's just been unembraced and demoted. It's no wonder life feels reactive and combative and divisive. And no wonder we don't see the sacred, or the holy, or the opportunities to heal the parts that have been diminished and wounded. But that sufficiency at our core—our capacity to be penny-finder, grace-spiller, and healer—gives us purpose.

Back to the story. It's as if the little girl in the story is swimming in a sea of grace, and in her heart and mind, that sea is available to everyone. You see, the penny is a paradigm. And here's our question today: What paradigm owns me?

Here are my pennies:

- God is alive and well in everyday life and in the people around me.
- The ordinary is the hiding place for the holy.
- In small gifts and gestures, we find ourselves celebrating the sacrament of the present.
- In honoring grace, I say yes to sanctuary, wholeness, resilience, unity, inclusiveness, and healing.

And here's the good news: This isn't an assignment. It's the permission to draw on the reservoir that is already inside: the gift of enough. Granted, in troubled times, it doesn't feel easy to access.

So, here is our invitation today: Share your delight (your discovered penny) with someone else. We can risk living less-than-tidy lives. We can risk asking for less than perfection from others (and ourselves). We can risk loving. In a glance, in a word, in a touch, in a gesture, there is healing and kindness and hope; the permission to dance is offered. We cannot change the pain in our lives or the lives of others. But we can accompany each other, and, along the way, look for pennies.

Today, I spent a little time raking big-leaf maple leaves, some of them up to fourteen inches across. I had to stop raking just to admire them. "Look," I say to the sky, "I found another penny!"

Chapter Twenty-Three

How We Live Makes a Difference

"Remember, if someone dances with you in the rain, they will most certainly walk with you in a storm," I tell the sheep this morning. "So, thank you for listening to me every week. I am grateful." Their look tells me, "No worries, that's what we're good at."

"My world shook a little yesterday," I tell them. "My father died."

Rest in peace, Jerry Hershey. I'm glad you were my dad. Today, I'm remembering and telling stories.

—November 16, 2020

I've told this story before, but want to tell it again to honor my father. I am the son of a brick mason. I am the eldest of five children. Which means that my summer options, as a schoolboy, were limited. I could be a hod carrier (mixing mortar—called "mud"—hauling bricks, blocks or stone and intuiting the needs of masons not known for their patience).

Or, I could be a hod carrier.

Being a hod carrier is real work. I mean, physical work. Dog-tired at the end of the day work. And I couldn't wait to grow up and go to college, and get a real job.

My father's leadership style, typical of Midwestern fathers of his generation, was straightforward, "Don't loaf. Don't whine. Don't make excuses. This'll make a man out of you." (I will admit, as a high school football player and wrestler, I couldn't have asked for a better workout regimen.)

Even so, college beckoned. Real work, you know, where I could make a real difference. And become somebody.

And I did. After two degrees and an ordination, I set out as The Reverend. No longer just a hod carrier, or just a construction worker.

On one visit to Michigan in my late thirties, my father and I drove the streets in the small town of Sturgis, drifting in his pickup truck. We could drive for miles without saying much. (Not a bad skill to learn.) The truck slowed as if by volition, and I wondered if something was amiss. Then it hit me. My father slowed to regard a house that he had built decades prior. He parked by the curb. And he told me stories about building the house, about the owner, about members of the crew, and about pranks played on the job site.

For the rest of the afternoon, we meandered the streets, looking not just at houses or chimneys, but also at the quality of work that has stood the test of time. These weren't just buildings. They were works of art and labors of love.

And then we stopped in front of a house I recognized. Where I spent a summer on a crew, just a hod carrier, building someone's dream. (But I hadn't seen it.) And the light bulb came on. Now, I never use the phrase "just a" anymore. About anyone.

I know this for certain: it doesn't take much to nurse resentment or regret. There are times when whatever we are doing seems not enough (no doubt a miasma of guilt or shame and the vagaries of public opinion).

Italian psychiatrist Roberto Assagioli tells a parable about three stonecutters working on a cathedral, set in the Middle Ages. Each is asked what he is doing. The first responds angrily, "Idiot! Use your eyes! They bring me a rock, I cut it into a block, they take it away, and they bring me another rock. I've been doing this since I was a boy, and I'm going to be doing it until the day I die."

The second man smiles warmly and says, "I'm earning a living for my beloved family. With my wages I have built a home, there is food on our table, the children are growing strong."

The third man pauses, and with a look of deep fulfillment says, "I am building a great cathedral. It will be a holy lighthouse where people lost in the dark can find their strength and remember their way. And it will stand for a thousand years!"

Not everyone feels the nobility of the third stonecutter. Or the selflessness of the second. But we have all felt the heaviness or bleakness of the first. To wonder, does any of what I do make a difference? Let's be clear: the parable is not simply about work. The parable is about how we derive our value-—our self-worth and our dignity and our calling—and how that spills onto everything we do, and everything we touch, and every person whose path we cross.

Over the years I have heard, "I'm just a volunteer (or just a member, or catechist, or aide, or worker, or helper, or employee, or friend or mother or fill in the blank)."

To each I say, No. You see, "just a" creates a label and tells us what we are not. And when we label, we dismiss. (Regardless of the label. Dorothy Day once scoffed, "Don't call me a saint. I don't want to be dismissed so easily.")

So, how then do we make a difference? Your work (labor) is your turf of responsibility. Which is only part of our DNA. Because no matter where we labor or toil, our calling is to spill the light. And the good news? For this we don't have to pass a test, or qualify; we have only to be willing. Jesus made it simple, "Let your light shine." Not, when you get your act together. Not, when you feel noble. Not, when you find a specific vocation. Not, after you've chased all the gloom away. Just let it shine. Because the light is already there. Inside of you. Now.

My father never signed a contract. His handshake was his word. One man told me, "When Jerry Hershey shook your hand you knew you were going to get something you would be proud of. Something that would stand the test of time."

What did my father build? Houses.

What did my father do? He made a difference.

It doesn't take much to cover our light with a bushel. And there's a whole lot of fear and worry and apprehension and hurry and the need for perfection that can do the job. But what we do, and who we are, touches lives, plain and simple. This matters more than ever, in a divisive world, a world on edge, a world where a kind word or gesture makes all the difference.

So, what if we let our light shine? What if we build a world where people matter? Where humanity blossoms, permeating inclusion and dignity and mercy and creativity and kindness and magnanimity and hope. Where we walk the earth each day in search of good deeds and acts to carry out. Because how we live makes a difference.

Chapter Twenty-Four

This Moment Matters

"Holiday plans are a little catawampus," I tell the sheep.

"What are holiday plans?" one asks.

"When you have a whole lot up in the air, you try to make plans," I explain.

"Do you have any plans?" another asks.

"Well, not really. But it sounds a whole lot better if you make something up when you are asked."

"So, what people think is more important than having plans?"

"Yes, something like that."

—November 23, 2020

There are articles and stories aplenty about how we navigate this "return to normal." How do we make choices about what we honor? (This is true: If we don't choose, the choice is made for us by default.) I've talked with some who already feel thrown back into a whirlwind world.

I overheard one woman tell a friend, "All I wanted was a weekend of self-care. Is that too much to ask? Oh, well. Maybe next time." It sounded familiar and I smile, because nothing says self-care like consternation and giving yourself grief for missing the mark. We have forgotten how to be gentle with ourselves, making space for a whole heart, surprised by wonder and grace.

Here's what I know: During this shift, as "normal" life is reframed. I want to tend to my heart.

This means that there is a place I will choose to visit from time to time, a place called Enough:

- that place where the heart slows,
- where gratitude spills,
- where we can touch the root of inner wisdom (a taproot some call the soul),
- where we are not afraid or adversarial,
- where we do not need to shy away from sorrow or disappointment,
- where grace is alive.

Betty taught me this. Betty was a character. A member of a writing group I enjoyed hanging out with some time ago. Betty was inimitable and full of spunk and verve. She had raised her children on a fishing boat in Alaska. She was the age where it's not helpful to guess or ask (but I'm guessing a good bit north of eighty). Now living in West Seattle, she invited me to visit her garden, a small lot behind her home.

"Come here," she says, and we walked down the back steps. "I gotta show you something."

"Yes, Ma'am," I say, smiling.

You know how when you create a garden, you begin with a path that is at least three feet in width? And over time, as plants encroach, the path narrows? Betty's is wide enough for us to put one foot in front of the other. Each side of the pathway is lined with large pots, filled with plants spilling. As a garden designer, my mind is spinning, and I'm thinking, "I can fix this! I can help Betty."

We get to the back of her lot. Around the corner at the edge of her garage is an old wicker chair.

"This is it," she tells me. "It's my 'when the world pisses me off' chair."

I'm still grinning, and I'm thinking, *Now, that is a great name.*

"Whenever I need time to regroup, I come sit in my chair," Betty says.

And I'm thinking, "I get it. But why is it back here in the corner?" And then it occurs to me: Surrounding the chair is a garage wall and the neighbor's tall fence covered with climbing flowers. This is Betty's sanctuary. This is a place called Enough.

We're walking back toward the house. And I'm about to give her advice that will improve her garden. She'll be soooo grateful. And she asks, "Did you notice the plants along the pathway?" I bite my tongue.

"I hope so," she continues. "They're all my favorite herbs. By the time I get to my chair my jeans are covered with the fragrance of the herbs."

I smile from ear to ear every time I think of my afternoon with Betty. It does my heart good. You see, here's what Betty knew: This moment matters.

This is important. Sanctuary is not withdrawal for withdrawal sake. It's about permission to pay attention to (to honor) what really matters. If we do not, we concede attention to that which assaults us by default.

This moment matters.

When I was a boy, stories from the Bible were a staple in my education. Remember the Old Testament story about Moses, on a mountain in a desolate place, on the edge of gloom? A bush begins to burn. And a voice speaks from that burning bush. "Take off your shoes," it said. "You are on holy ground."

Now, in the church of my youth, this was not a suggestion. This was God, after all, so it was a command, to be broken at great peril. Because, if God is holy, show some respect. If not, you're going to get smote. (I can still hear the severe tone in our pastor's voice. This taking the shoes off wasn't meant to make us smile.)

I now believe that those words were not a command at all. I believe they were an invitation. Permission. You are on holy ground. Wow.

Therefore, in order to touch, to feel this ground, let's remove whatever blocks or inhibits or prevents. Take off your shoes. Savor the ground. Jeans covered with herbs. Savor the ground. Grounded…literally sinking into life.

Sanctuary does not remove us from life. But it allows us to be fully alive smack-dab in the middle. The parable of the mustard seed from Mark's Gospel reminds us that our impulse or temptation to control the garden will always get us in trouble. When tidiness is our primary goal, we tend to miss the miracles along the way.

This moment matters.

Chapter Twenty-Five

L'Envoi

"I'm saying goodbye," I tell the sheep. "This will be my last Sunday with you all.

They look, but say nothing, maybe waiting for a punch line.

"I know, I wanted to tell you sooner, but there's been a lot on my plate. I will be saying goodbye to Vashon Island. I will be saying goodbye to my home and garden, and moving to another part of Washington state."

"OK," their look tells me, "now I see why it wasn't easy."

I stand for a while. This morning, the fog is thick, as if gently holding our emotions in place.

"I will miss you," I tell them. "You helped me make it through this year. You have no idea."

As I walk away, I think I hear one say, "Just so you know, you're our favorite preacher." And that did my heart good.

—November 30, 2020

To say "2020 was a year of significant change" is to utter a sentence with zero hyperbole. Life-altering for too many. And yet, it's not change so much as uncertainty that unnerves us, is it?

I think because of some ingrained lure to find closure and make sense of it all. Not knowing what's next isn't the kind of fun we had in mind. Of course, the way we frame life and circumstance is curious and makes a difference. Because when keeping score matters, we're not able to embrace our vulnerability and fragility and the way they introduce us to what is strong and sufficient on the inside.

Today, can I allow the gift of life (the sacred in the ordinary present) to be enough?

Someone asked, "So, you're no longer a gardener?"

Well, it's true that I will no longer have a garden. But at my core, I am (and will always be) a gardener. Because people who love this world, people who pay attention, are gardeners, whether or not they have ever picked up a trowel.

Because gardening is not just about digging. Or planting for that matter. Gardening is about cherishing. And to cherish, we must be present. The garden is my teacher. And a wondrous and incurable obsession, which takes you meandering to garden paths. Just for the sake of meandering. Of course, the obsessed tend toward jealous excess. I will be unable to hide my proclivity for the sacred necessity of Adirondack chairs, my infatuation with old garden roses, my enchantment with early summer's butterfly cabaret, or my distrust of anyone who is put off by dirty fingernails. Just so you are forewarned. And that, will never change.

Now it is time for what is next. "And suddenly you know," Meister Eckhart wrote (I am certain just to encourage me), "It's time to start something new and trust the magic of beginnings." I know that the magic is in the invitation.

First, though, the invitation to pause, to take time to reexamine our priorities and recall what we treasure most. To ask questions about what really matters. It's not the labels we wear, or the address, vocation, or prefix in front of your name. It's about the kind of people we want to be. Peace, reconciliation, forgiveness, rediscovering charity, and finding ways to grieve keep us spiritually hydrated. And radical kindness always matters.

Here is what I know: I want to be a dispenser and bestower of grace. Your well-being matters to me. Because we need one another. No one of us is on this journey alone. Let us together build sanctuaries of empathy and humility.

When we are disconnected from the sacrament of the present, and from the gift of Enough, we disconnect from ourselves, and we need a reset button. Each button a way of saying: It wouldn't be a bad idea for our well-being if we quit keeping score in order to remember what really matters.

It's never easy to admit when the load you carry is heavy, in part because so many are carrying much, much heavier loads. And I don't want to make a fuss. But my spirit knows I've been lugging a lot, and I shake my head, knowing that I don't give myself the permission to set that stuff down and to take nourishment. It's been one of my lifelong wrestling matches.

It doesn't help to add the obligation of a list. Because this I do know: Though I do want to travel lighter, it seems contradictory—only exacerbating the problem—to add another to-do list to the menu necessary to live this life fully alive. And, yes, we can get oddly grandiose about this whole state of affairs. We can turn loving life into another contest. You know, if we're going to try this on for size (living the sacrament of the present), we might as well excel at it, as if we can become some sort of expert at loving life or productive stillness. You never know who might notice.

Every time we add the compulsion, we reinforce the discomfiting implication that this day, as it currently stacks up, is not sufficient. It needs to be improved upon, made more respectable or enviable by some gadget or self-help course available for only three low monthly payments on our credit card.

I love Lynne Twist's reminder, "The problem is not simply that we work too much, the problem is that we are working for the wrong reward... We are paid in the wrong currency. What if we were to expand our definition of wealth to include those things that grow only in time—time to walk in the park, time to take a nap, time to play with children, to read a good book, to dance, to put our hands in the garden, to cook playful meals with friends, to paint, to sing, to meditate, to keep a journal."

Gratefully and gladly, the full force of life and the gift of Enough usually envelop me when I'm looking the other way: looking, say, for answers or magic or resolve (maybe a reprieve from the disquiet of moving). It is a lot like grace in that way. It enters in, slows the heartbeat, and before you know it, you're sitting still. Relishing, contemplating, savoring, and just being, if only for a moment. These moments reintroduce me to a world that is antithetical to the world that tells me the five (or seven or ten) things I must do to get past, or get over, or stay on top.

For me, it happened on Saturday, my final day on Vashon Island. On this early December day, the sun graces us, now lower in the sky, with shafts (marionettes) of light, messages of hope through the cathedral of trees. Lord, have mercy. I walk the garden slowly, as a prayer.

Just off the back patio, resilient blooms on Mary Rose. They are Advent candles for peace. It makes me smile real big.

Much of the garden is all cheerfully, though terribly sprawled, flopped, and askew. Winter is around the corner. Nuthatches and chickadees continue their resolute forays to the feeder. When I look up, an occasional wispy cloud rides a river through the southern sky like a backdrop which has missed its cue and is hastily escorted across the stage. The air is touched with the smoke of wood stoves. And except for the nuthatches and an occasional stirring of our wooden wind chimes, there is silence.

People who love life embrace particularity. Particularity means not shying away from the detail. In fact, particularity throws caution to the wind and jumps, whole-hog, into the fray of details. It's about awareness: noting the specifics, slowing us down, and immersing us in the full weight, the density of the daily and the ordinary. Yes, the ordinary, the hiding place for the holy.

This year has rocked all of our worlds. But even with all the upheaval, there is the benefit of a reset button as we walk one another home. To remember what we may have lost, but also the permission to live with a soft heart. To create places for sanctuary, empathy, inclusion, compassion, and kindness, spaces where we are refueled to make a difference.

About the Author

Terry Hershey is an author, humorist, inspirational speaker, dad, ordained minister, golf addict, and smitten by French wine. He is the author of *This Is the Life: Mindfulness, Finding Grace, and the Power of the Present Moment*, *Soul Gardening*, *Sanctuary*, and *The Power of Pause*. He divides his time between designing sanctuary gardens and sharing his practice of mindfulness and savoring this life. He lives in Port Ludlow, Washington.